What To Do When You Don't Know What To Do

Building a Pyramid of Interventions

By
Margaret A. Searle

With
Dr. Karen Ackerman-Spain

Copyright © 2007, Searle Enterprises, Inc.

ISBN 978-0-9796088-0-3

LCCN 2007903013

Cover art by Morgan L. Searle

All rights reserved. No part of this book may be reproduced or transmitted in any form or by any means, electronic or mechanical, including photocopying, recording, or by information storage and retrieval systems, without the written permission of the publisher, except by a reviewer who may quote brief passages in a review.

Printed in the United States of America

To Michael, my husband, business partner, encourager, supporter, and very best friend. Your kindness, humor, and wisdom make what seems impossible, possible.

Table of Contents

Acknowledgments

To my children, Morgan and Kenton, who encouraged me and tried to keep the noise and activity levels reasonable when I needed to think; Mary West, the kind of mother whose "go for it" attitude always made us believe in our dreams; my writing partner, Dr. Karen Ackerman-Spain, who has the unique ability to make even the toughest day of research and brainstorming fun; my friends and colleagues Joan Love, Mary Jane Roberts, Marilyn Swartz, Deb Siegel, Deb McDaniel, Jeff Williams, my niece Jessica Stevens, my sister-in-law Alicia Searle, and my sister Connie Knight who added their insights and energy to this project.

This problem-solving system has been a growing, changing design. It is the result of constant feedback and ideas shared over the years as teachers and administrators throughout Ohio taught me as much as I taught them in every seminar I conducted. A special thanks to the faculty of Solon City Schools as they allowed me to practice on them as we refined the model together.

Introduction

What To Do When You Don't Know What To Do

Building a Pyramid of Interventions

Sonya is trying hard but just cannot seem to remember much about what we did yesterday. Robert is out of his seat again, vying for attention by bothering Trina. Frank is staring out of the window when he should be reading his book. Juanita just snapped her pencil in two and called Tony a jerk. No wonder these kids don't get their work completed. They are all having a hard time feeling successful in school. Each one has a unique learning barrier and a different way of demonstrating the frustrations they feel.

Discovering what is causing each student's problems and then engaging school personnel, the family, and the student in the job of agreeing upon the best ways to support each other's efforts in problem-solving is the purpose of this book.

In order to get the best results, home and school must work together to establish the right conditions for success. Maintaining the belief that each student and adult is knowledgeable, capable, and willing to learn, even if everything about their behavior indicates they are not, is one key to successful problem-solving. Taking the attitude that a given teacher will never change or a specific student just doesn't care will only result in feelings of helplessness and lack of action. Having the belief that there *is* a hot button that is capable of turning failure into success is fundamental to being successful. The hard part is finding that hot button.

Some people think that testing and labeling a student is the hot button. I have heard teachers say, "Why are we wasting time doing all these interventions when we know this kid needs to be tested?" The belief underlying this statement is that testing and placement *is* an intervention. It is not. Labeling only gives the problem a name, and placement just moves the problem to a new location. It takes more than that to make a difference for a student. The real hot button is a focused quality plan that is carefully monitored and continually adjusted until the child is finally successful.

Having a specialist help the student certainly makes sense to most of us, but the intensive one-on-one help general education teachers envision in the special education rooms is typically a myth. The reality is that most interventionists are attempting to serve a wider range of high-needs students than the general education teachers. In addition, the nature of special education scheduling and class structures often makes the amount of one-on-one support fairly minimal. Too often the type of support is simply help with assignments, homework, and testing rather than specific interventions targeting the root causes of the student's problems. The old model results in an increasingly widening gap in achievement as the student gets older. We need a new approach.

Although there are appropriate times to address disabilities by putting an Individual Educational Plan (IEP) in place, labeling too early often slows down the process of identifying quality interventions. This is due to the fact that there is a tendency to assume all students with a given label are struggling with the same issues. I will use a medical analogy to illustrate this point. In a doctor's office, as we describe our symptoms of headache and fever, a physician may assume we have the flu. Even though flu is often the cause of these symptoms, it doesn't necessarily mean it is this time. Being open to data that might suggest other possibilities is critical to effective diagnosis in both medicine and education. Effectively diagnosing and then carefully prescribing treatments that are matched to the uniqueness of the individual's specific needs is essential to success.

In each chapter of this book, I will elaborate on ways to diagnose causes of student problems and prescribe effective interventions using a nine-step problem-solving system. I will start by spelling out the specifics of each of the nine steps of the process in Chapter One. The other chapters will use case studies to give more specific practice and examples for applying the three key skills of the process: analyzing with the "Five Reasons Deep" process, setting DATA goals, and developing a continuum of interventions.

Chapter One will give a complete overview of the problem-solving steps. It will spell out the roles and responsibilities of both the coach and the team members who attend the problem-solving meeting. Basic guidelines for ensuring the positive environment necessary for collaboration will be listed as well as reasons and guidelines for effective family involvement.

Chapter Two will elaborate on what happens during the coaching process that takes place before the problem-solving meeting. Trying to solve problems without knowing the root causes wastes time and frustrates everyone. This chapter will provide short case studies to provide practice opportunities in using the "Five Reasons" analysis that uncover root causes. Once root causes are identified, specific practice on setting DATA goals is provided. This sets the stage for enabling the problem-solving team to do the work of coming up with a tailor-made plan to support the student. The clearer the DATA goal, the more likely it is that correct interventions and accommodations will be put in place.

Chapter Three provides lists of ideas often called the "universal interventions." This is the beginning part of a system called Response to Intervention (RtI), which is consistent with the Individuals with Disabilities Education Improvement Act (IDEIA), 2004. You might think of these universal strategies as the "ounce of prevention" or they may be the first step in the cure. These Tier I interventions can be put in place for a struggling student but have been shown to be beneficial to all types of learners in any type of classroom.

Chapter Four is a series of case studies that apply Tier I, II, and III interventions for students with more intense needs than those of typical learners. Using many research-based ideas, this chapter suggests a continuum of specific strategies that could be helpful for a variety of cases. In each case, the intervention plans start with a clear goal and then use the least intrusive level of intervention the team believes will produce acceptable growth. As data indicates lower Tier interventions to be ineffective, the plan is changed, modified, or replaced by more intense interventions. Some cases in this chapter will describe how students who once needed high-intensity levels worked their way down the continuum as they showed improvement in skills and self-monitoring. The goal for each student is to work as far down the Tiers as possible in order to become more independent as well as successful with the new skills.

RtI is a way of adjusting the environment and instruction based upon the individual student's response to an intervention plan. This adjustment process is guided by a multi-tier system of options (Tier I, II and III). The RtI system makes decisions about learner needs using research-based approaches that are carefully monitored and documented.

Tier I interventions are differentiated instructional practices that meet a broad range of student needs in the general education classroom. Tier II interventions are designed to be more intensive than Tier I. This level often provides supplemental services that work in tandem with the Tier I strategies. These interventions are designed to give students the extra boost they need in order to transfer newly learned skills to the general education environment. Tier III provides the most intensive interventions. This level calls for treatments that are different from those that can be accomplished in a general education classroom. These interventions are research-based treatments that may be provided by any number of specialists such as community agencies, Title I specialists, speech therapists, remedial and special education interventionists, counselors, psychologists . . .

Even when interventions are based upon research, we must be cautious about jumping to the "silver bullet" conclusion. Research is ever-evolving. What seems true today may need to be adjusted as we uncover new findings about how children learn. Also, a successful intervention plan for one student may not be successful for another with the exact same symptoms. This is why the careful monitoring and feedback of any intervention plan is of critical importance. If a student fails to show a positive response to a given intervention, timely adjustments to the plan need to be made.

This problem-solving model is not about going through the motions or steps of a process. This is about changing the lives of students, one small step at a time. If the evidence from your intervention plan does not clearly show positive movement, the plan must be changed or replaced. This process goes on until the student succeeds or graduates, whichever comes first. We never give up! The Sonyas, Roberts, Franks, and Juanitas of our world are counting on us.

NOTE:

The "Five Reasons Deep" process is based upon the strategy of "Five Whys" referred to in the book *The Fifth Dimension* by Peter Senge.

Chapter One
Why Do We Need A New Approach?

Jessie is an attractive, intelligent high school sophomore who has developed an intense dislike for school. Her parents have exhausted their emotional resources trying to figure out why Jessie, who is a good reader, cannot seem to make passing grades. This downward spiral of hating school because she is not successful and not being successful because she hates it appears to be an endless cycle of hopelessness. Now the school is calling to schedule a conference:

> *Today I received the dreaded call from school. They want us to come in for another meeting. I don't know why we have to meet again. It's not like I can't cite chapter and verse what they have told us over and over. We go in; the teachers take turns going around the table confessing my child's sins and shortcomings. We know her work is far below where it should be, and her frustrations are often displayed as discipline problems. I know the teachers are frustrated, but so are we. Why can't any of us seem to help her? Even though we are doing the very best we know how, we leave the school feeling like inferior parents. Now they want to test her and put her in special education. My heart is just breaking.*

Wouldn't it be better if this parent experienced this?

> *My daughter's teacher called today to invite us to a new kind of meeting. Mrs. Swartz said that in this meeting we will not be discussing a list of Jessie's problems or things that have happened in the past. The meeting is focused only on what to do to help her. By the end of the meeting, we will have a very specific plan for helping our daughter with one or two key issues. When we lick those problems, we'll take on others until we turn this pattern of poor performance around. How refreshing!*
>
> *The "we" part of this meeting is scary, though. I definitely got the impression that my husband and I are going to be given a key part in this plan. I'm not trained to teach math. In fact, I'm not very good at math myself, but the teacher assures me that we will not be assigned anything we don't feel comfortable doing. I guess we'll see.*

Having Jessie at the meeting is a worry. She doesn't need another kick in the teeth. Mrs. Swartz assured me that the rules of these meetings strictly forbid any form of "admiring the problem" or blaming. One hundred percent of the meeting time is to be spent talking about ways to support Jessie from both home and school. That certainly will be a new kind of meeting. If Mrs. Swartz is true to her word, we just might have a chance of preventing Jessie from eventually dropping out of school.

Changes in thinking for a collaborative problem-solving model:

Traditional Approach	This Approach
• Goal: placement in a special program	• Goal: find interventions that work for the student
• Testing provides a label for the student	• The process provides data that results in a specific plan of intervention
• Study and discuss a list of problem areas	• Study and discuss interventions
• Get permission from the parent to test	• Involve the home in developing solutions
• Do this *to* the student	• *Involve* the student in the process
• Core group of faculty members are expected to have the solutions for every case	• Flexible group of ad hoc "experts" are selected based upon needs of each case

For years research and professional literature have strongly supported having students with disabilities learn with their non-disabled peers.

For years, research and professional literature have strongly supported having students with disabilities learn with their non-disabled peers. In many schools, however, this practice is a partial reality at best. Some schools ignore the data showing that when high-risk students are tracked with each other, the gap gets wider and wider every year. Dumping these students into general education rooms without the proper support plan is just as damaging.

Every teacher I've ever talked to has agreed that there are children in general education rooms who are worse off than many of the students with IEPs (Individualized Education Plans). These schools are asking the question, "Why are we waiting for a label to get help for these kids?"

This chapter will suggest specific steps and procedures that address ways to change the old approach to a new problem-solving system for students experiencing difficulty. This model recruits members of the faculty who have good rapport and listening skills to be trained as coaches for problem-solving. These fellow teachers, counselors and psychologists act as sounding boards and guides during the referral process. Their job is to help the referring teachers unravel the symptoms of problems in order to see what root causes lie beneath. This analytical process leads to a clear focus on a high-impact but narrow goal for the student. Once this goal setting is done, a team of experts from the faculty works in tandem with the student and the student's family in coming up with targeted and effective interventions.

The Problem-Solving Process Checklist

Before the problem-solving meeting:

- ❑ Teacher makes an appointment to see a coach.
- ❑ Teacher gathers available data on the student.
    - ❑ Work samples
    - ❑ Grades
    - ❑ Attendance
    - ❑ Cum file information
    - ❑ Other information as needed

During the referral conference:

- ❑ Create "Strengths and Concerns" lists.
- ❑ Conduct "Five Reasons Deep."
- ❑ Decide upon baseline information.
- ❑ Set a DATA Goal and data-collection strategy.
- ❑ Select the team for the meeting.
- ❑ Decide who will prepare the parent for the meeting.
- ❑ Decide who will make the follow-up call to the parent.
- ❑ Decide who will prepare the student for the meeting.
- ❑ Set the proposed meeting time.

- ❑ Prepare the student for the meeting.
- ❑ Prepare the parent for the meeting.
- ❑ Give the rest of the team the Baseline form and other information to help them develop at least three tailor-made interventions (one for home, one for school, and one for the student).

Problem-solving meeting and follow-up:

- ❑ Hold the meeting to create a plan.
- ❑ Document responses and evaluate the effectiveness of the plan.
- ❑ Hold follow-up meetings to revise and refine the plan.

Who is the Coach?

The ideal would be to have every person on the staff become proficient at using the coaching skills.

Many times, schools start out using administrators, psychologists, and counselors as coaches. They then add special education teachers and general education teachers who show an interest in learning the coaching skills. The ideal would be to have every person on the staff become proficient at using the coaching skills.

Referral coaches should be selected based upon their:

- earned respect from the staff due to their skill and good judgment;
- ability to establish and maintain a positive working relationship with staff, parents, and students;
- ability and willingness to communicate and collaborate.

What Happens at the Referral Conference?

Purpose: To assist the referring person (teacher, parent, or student) in identifying the root causes and help develop a clear and specific DATA goal that will guide the entire intervention process.

Who: Typically the classroom teacher makes the referral but other faculty members, parents/guardians or the student himself may do this. The process is then guided with the help of one or two trained staff members who coach the referring person.

Time: With a trained coach and faculty, the referral conference generally takes less than forty minutes. In the beginning stages, it can take a bit longer.

Since it takes just as much time and energy to work on the wrong problem as it does the right one, the intention of the **referral conference** is to make certain everyone is focused on root causes, not just symptoms. In this system, the person making the referral (teacher, parent or student) is put in touch with a referral coach—a person on the faculty who has been trained in active listening and diagnostic questioning. This happens **before a formal problem-solving meeting** is scheduled. The coach guides the analytical discussion to identify the root causes and then assists in designing a DATA goal, a specific, short-term, measurable target for change. (See Chapter 2.)

At first, this process may seem like a time consuming step. In the long run, it saves time by narrowing the scope of the problem-solving

D	What adults do Differently
A	What the student will Achieve
T	In what amount of Time
A	as Assessed by . . .

meeting and making certain that simply "admiring the problem" doesn't happen. Team members come to the meeting prepared with powerful suggestions targeted at a very specific improvement goal. This is key to keeping the entire meeting short, positive and productive.

Where do we begin?

In the first of the nine steps, the coach and teacher meet to identify the academic and behavioral concerns and the student strengths. The list of strengths tells what the student brings to the process and gives us a good place to start.

Example of the process:

Referral Step 1

The teacher, Mr. Lummer, went to the coach to get help for Rhonda's reading and writing problems. Rhonda is a bright eighth grader who easily reads the words on the page but gets to the end and has no clue what it said. Her written responses are short, and her penmanship needs a code breaker to read it. (Coach takes minutes on the **Strengths and Concerns** Form during the conference).

Strengths and Concerns Interview

Academic Concerns:	**Behavior Concerns:**

Strengths to build on:

Referral Step 2

The coach noted **baseline data** on Rhonda based upon Mr. Lummer's grades, her work samples, and data from past years. This step continues to emerge throughout the process (Baseline and Planning Form–Chapter 2)

Baseline Data and Planning Form

Student Name ____________ Date referred __________ Referring person(s) ____________

Steps 1 & 2 - Key issues to be addressed*:

Step 3 - Baseline data:**

Frequency:

Severity:

Places problem is observed:

Times when problem is observed:

Things that trigger the problem:

Strategies that resulted in positive response:

Strategies found to be ineffective:

Reinforcements found to be effective:

Reinforcements not recommended:

Step 4 - DATA Goal***:

Step 5 - Team members:

Step 6 - Who will contact parents?

Step 7 - Who will make the follow-up call?

Step 8 - Who will prepare the student?

Referral taken by ____________

*Attach Strengths and Concerns form ** Attach work samples and observation data *** See "Five Reasons" document

Referral Step 3

The coach and Mr. Lummer **analyzed the key concerns** and decided that Rhonda was "not focusing and not linking what she reads to her prior knowledge." These are two root causes for Rhonda's comprehension problems.

Referral Step 4

They **wrote a DATA goal** in order to focus the team's attention on very specific aspects of Rhonda's reading. Each member of the team will now design interventions to achieve this targeted area.

Referral Step 5

The next step was to **select staff experts** to make up the team for addressing this DATA goal. Because they had set up a pool of "problem-solving experts" in this school, the coach and teacher were able to select just the right people for this case. They chose seven members: the remedial reading teacher, last year's teacher, Mr. Lummer, the parents, Rhonda, and the building administrator.

The Pool of Problem-Solving Experts

Does this sound familiar?

Teacher 1: *"I made a referral to get help for James weeks ago, and I haven't heard a thing. James could have his AARP card before he comes to the top of that list. What's the deal with this time lag?"*

Teacher 2: *"I don't know why you're getting all bent out of shape about the time. For one thing, there are only five members on that team, and they can only do so much. For another thing, when you get to the meeting they'll just tell you to do a bunch of stuff you've probably already tried and already know doesn't work. It's not like they'll give you a gold mine of unique ideas."*

These issues are not uncommon complaints. Fortunately, a few minor adjustments to the team make-up can reduce the severity of these problems.

Getting rid of weak interventions can be addressed by forming an "expert pool"

Getting rid of the time lag

My faculty made a list of issues that tended to come up over and over in our meetings (see below). Every staff member was then asked to select one issue on which to become our resident problem-solving expert. These people would become familiar with the research and develop a deep continuum of powerful interventions in one area. It was my job as the administrator to support them in developing these new skills (i.e., link them to other teachers with expertise, send them to conferences, buy books and tapes on their topics, coordinate efforts to find articles and other resources on the topics). This did more to upgrade our level of service and feelings of professionalism than anything else we did.

This "pool of problem-solving experts" approach allowed us to put together tailor-made teams for each case. The burden of coming up with powerful interventions didn't continuously fall to the same small group of people. Sharing the responsibility allowed us to schedule several meetings simultaneously, if needed. In this way, more cases were addressed in a shorter amount of time.

Our list of expert areas:

Reading decoding	Math concepts	Attention span	Disruptive
Reading comprehension	Math skills	Motivation	Bullying
Reading in the content area	Impulsivity	Aggressive	Social misfit
Organization problems	Writing	Phobias	Self-abuse
Oral expression	Hearing problems	Absenteeism	Withdrawn
Group work issues	Hyperactivity	Visual problems	Memory

Selecting Team Members for the Meeting:

1) The **size and make-up of the team** for the problem-solving meeting will vary with the case. Five to seven people work well. There is nothing more unnerving for a parent or student than walking into a roomful of a dozen people and feeling on the spot.
2) Some schools use core members for consistency and add experts as needed. Although there are advantages to having consistent and well-trained members on the team, using *only* core members can limit expertise and growth opportunities for others. It also wears out the core team and/or limits the number of students who can be served. A professional development goal should be to increase the numbers of staff who are available and comfortable in serving as the "**problem-solving experts**" for a wide variety of cases.
3) Team members should be selected based upon their:
    - personal expertise for the type of interventions needed;
    - willingness to do research to develop skill in their chosen area;
    - ability to establish and maintain a positive working environment;
    - ability and willingness to communicate and collaborate;
    - willingness to learn and use active listening skills, diagnostic questioning, research-based interventions, and ways of tracking and reporting student progress.

Everyone in the room is to be an active part of the team, focusing on solutions.

4) The administrator should see that all faculty members are trained in meeting roles, responsibilities, and procedures before being invited to attend. Everyone is expected to bring three interventions to the meeting that will help the student reach the DATA goal: one for home, one for school, and one for the student to use. Everyone in the room is to be an active part of the team, focusing on solutions.

What does the team look like?

Who	Role/purpose on team	Checklist of Responsibilities
Administrator	Facilitate communication, allocate resources, maintain a welcoming and safe environment, support and monitor implementation, maintain documentation	Contribute at least three intervention ideas at all meetings May serve as student advocate* May make the follow-up call to parent* May serve as coach*
Referring Person	Get assistance for analyzing, developing and/or implementing a continuum of ideas for meeting DATA goal. Collect data to determine the effectiveness of the plan.	Work with the coach to: Describe and diagnose key issues Set DATA goal using baseline data Select a tracking instrument Help select and notify team members May contact and prepare the parent* May act as the student advocate* Contribute at least three intervention ideas Implement interventions and track progress Analyze data in order to make decisions Maintain a welcoming environment
Referral Coach	Establish focus on a key issue Assist by helping the referring person see problems in a new light Give the teacher support during implementation of the intervention process.	Assist in focusing and diagnosing Help gather and/or organize baseline data Help select a tracking instrument Help select and notify team members May contact and prepare parent* May act as student advocate* May attend problem-solving meetings* Touch base between meetings to see if interventions are working Maintain a welcoming and safe environment during referral conferences
Other members Parent Student "Expert" staff Medical Social worker Psychologist Counselors Siblings Therapists Prior teachers Next year's teacher Interventionists Reading specialist Math specialist Tutors Instructional Aides Others as helpful	Provide a wide variety of of options for interventions and support, as needed.	Be familiar with the data before the meeting by using referral sheets or talking to the referring person. Prepare at least three intervention ideas that directly relate to the DATA goal: • one for the student to implement • one for home use • one for school personnel Maintain a welcoming and safe environment for everyone during meetings May act as the student advocate* Assist in implementation and/or follow-up meetings as requested (modeling, materials, data collection, additional interventions . . .) Assist in data analysis for making decisions at the follow-up meeting

*The person who assumes these roles may change to fit the needs of the case.

The Parent as a Team Member

Referral Step 6

Step 6 is deciding **who will assist the parent** in understanding the process. Hopefully, the teacher has already been communicating with the parents, so this is not the first time they have heard that there is a problem. Going to a formal meeting when parents don't know a problem exists tends to tick them off.

The referring teacher is generally the logical choice for making the call to set up the meeting. Teachers have the most information about the case, and they need to maintain control of the process. The only time it is unwise to have the teacher make the call to the parents is when the relationship has already been broken between this teacher and the family; then a more neutral person needs to step in and make the call.

During this call the following things should be discussed:

Checklist for conducting the parent call

1. The purpose of the meeting, as summarized by the DATA goal
2. Gathering data about strengths and concerns from the parents' viewpoint
3. The basic format, agenda and "Rules of the Road" that will guide the meeting
4. Scheduling of the meeting (date, time and place)
5. The assignment to bring three interventions that will help the student meet the DATA goal. (Everyone invited has this assignment.)
6. Who will be asked to serve on the team and why
7. The fact that someone will make a courtesy call within 48 hours to answer any questions or help them come up with interventions if they need it

The call might sound something like this:

Hello, Mr. O'Brien, this is Bart Lummer calling.

Hi, Bart. How are things going?

Actually, things are going pretty well. We are making progress with Rhonda's reading, but I think we have an opportunity to do more. I talked to a referral coach today, and we think there is a better approach to Rhonda's reading problem.

When you say referral coach, who are you talking about, exactly?

Purpose: Put the DATA goal in parent-friendly terms.

It's a faculty member who helps us analyze symptoms to find out what might be keeping us from solving problems with typical classroom strategies. In Rhonda's case we ended up thinking that focusing more intensely on helping Rhonda connect what she is reading to what she already knows might turn things around for her.

Well, I'm for anything that would help. It's hard to see her so frustrated.

Describe the meeting procedures.

Reducing frustration is exactly what our meeting will focus on. Each person invited to the meeting is asked to bring three ideas for helping Rhonda focus and connect better to what she is reading: one idea for the teachers to use in the classroom, one idea for you to use with Rhonda at home, and one idea for Rhonda to help herself. If every team member comes with three suggestions, we will have twenty-one suggestions in just a very few minutes.

You are going to give me twenty-one ideas that I should do at home?

No, only seven or so ideas will be in the "home column," and you and your wife may select any idea you are willing and able to do. I know you already help her a lot. This will just give you more possibilities to choose from. One of the ideas in the list will be your own suggestion, so you are guaranteed to have at least one idea on the list that you like.

Describe how this team is going to listen to each other and take action.

I'm supposed to bring ideas, too?

Yes, the family and the faculty are equal members on this team. We each have an opportunity to suggest things that could help Rhonda. We put everyone's ideas up on a chart in the proper columns, but each person chooses his or her own idea to actually implement.

I think I'm out of my league here. I could help you with your taxes, but I can't tell you how to teach reading.

Your suggestions don't have to be specific teaching ideas. You're the expert on your daughter's likes and dislikes, what might motivate her, and how we can make learning easier for her. Think back to your favorite teacher for ideas. What did he or she do that made you want to focus and read? Those ideas might work for Rhonda, too. We also have a list of ideas that other parents have suggested. Would you like to look that over?

Definitely, send the list.

Key to positive action

No talking about the problem, only discuss goals and solutions.

There is one more thing about this meeting that is very important.

What's that?

No one at the meeting is allowed to talk about any problems or concerns. We have to focus totally on the action plan for Rhonda. So if I slip up and bring up a missing assignment, you stop me. If you bring up a problem, I'll stop you. We can talk about problems afterward, but meeting time is sacred "do something about problems, don't just talk about them" time.

We could use that philosophy at my office.

Cover the who, what, when, where, and why of this meeting.

After setting the time and place and discussing who is on the team. . . .

I will send home the suggested idea list and Mrs. McDaniel, the principal, will call to see if you have any questions or concerns about the meeting. She can also help you with your ideas if you want her to. By the way, don't let the thought of bringing ideas keep you from coming to the meeting. We are interested in your advice, but it's no big deal if you don't want to give it.

Referral Step 7

Decide who will be the person to make the follow-up courtesy call. This may seem like a disposable step to some, but I have found that it accomplishes two things. The courtesy call emphasizes the importance of parent involvement and catches miscommunications and potential problems before they get out of hand.

When the school calls home, parents generally assume the worst: my child is sick, or she's in trouble again. This causes part of their listening skills to turn off. Many times, what the teacher thought was perfectly clear during the conversation was not. This follow-up call also short-circuits the problems that happen when dad is all "good-to-go" on the phone but when mom comes home she thinks the meeting is going to be another battle with the school. Now mom's either not coming, or she is coming ready to fight.

The courtesy call emphasizes the importance of parents being involved and catches miscommunications and potential problems before they get out of hand.

Student Involvement: Nothing About Me Without Me

Referral Step 8

Students who are at-risk not only need assistance and support with their difficulties, but also need adult modeling on the quality problem-solving processes. Every step of this process addresses this modeling in a very real and meaningful way. Involving students in team meetings accomplishes this goal by:

1. guiding the students in expressing their opinions about what the problem is and what could be causing it as well as what strengths they bring to the situation;
2. assisting them in seeing that everyone has problems and they are things that can be overcome and/or coped with;
3. helping students set their own goals to get the new and desired results;
4. considering alternatives before proceeding with selecting a plan;
5. honoring the student by giving them a voice in designing and selecting the plan;
6. assisting the student in collecting data that will serve as feedback on whether their choice of strategies is actually working;
7. helping students see that they are accountable for achieving the goals by helping adjust the plan as needed based upon data;
8. teaching children to ask for the resources and assistance they need.

Making the student feel respected instead of victimized by the process gets better cooperation.

A second goal is to make the student feel respected instead of victimized by the process. Including students in each step results in better cooperation as a result of their feeling that they have a say in what is being designed.

What does a student preparation conference look like?

In this case Rhonda's teacher has a good relationship with her, so he decides to be her advocate. Mr. Lummer goes over the purpose, procedures, and rules of the meeting. He then assists Rhonda in developing three good reading strategies which she will present at the meeting: one for home, one for school, and one for herself.

Purpose: Verify the DATA goal and get student commitment to work on it.

Hi, Rhonda. I want to talk to you about an idea I have for helping you improve your reading.

In a snotty voice, *"I can read just fine."*

Well, you do a great job at recognizing the words, but I've noticed you get to the bottom of the page and can't tell me what you've read.

Still cranky, *"So, who cares about reading this school stuff anyhow?"*

You might not care about school stuff but it will be a shame to have you fail your driver's test because you misread the questions, or get fired from your job because you couldn't read the memo from your boss.

Yeah, but I'm just not smart like the other kids. I read, and it never makes a darn bit of sense. It's just not gonna happen.

I think it can. All we have to do is teach you the tricks that some of the other kids have already figured out. You recognize the words already, so you're halfway there.

So what's this idea you have?

We have a team in the school to help brainstorm ideas that assist parents, kids and teachers to find new ways of tackling problems if the regular ways aren't working. I think we will be able to find a way that suits your style of learning to read.

What if they can't find a way to help?

We won't give up until we do. It's your job and my job to keep trying until we find something that does work.

So what do I have to do?

Everyone is an active member focused on solutions, not excuses or blaming.

Mr. Lummer goes over the meeting time, place, names of team members and why they were selected, as well as the fact that each team member has to bring three ideas for improving reading. This thought throws Rhonda.

You're kidding, right? I'm the one who can't read. How am I supposed to come up with three ideas?

I'll help you. First tell me any ideas that you think work for other people.

I don't know any.

All right, let me give you ideas, and you pick the ones you think sound like possibilities for you. Some kids never learn to pick out the most important ideas as they read. They think everything is important. We could work on that. We could also try what are called "Think alouds." That is where you and a partner read just one paragraph at a time and see if you agree on the main idea. This isn't so hard, because you can choose very short passages. You could even start with magazine articles on fashion or something else you like to read and then work on more difficult material once you get better at the skill. The third idea is a favorite of mine. It's called "argue with the author." In the margins, you write your opinions about what the author is saying. You can agree and praise the author's thoughts or challenge what the author is saying. Do any of those ideas appeal to you?

I like using the fashion magazine idea.

We could use fashion magazines for any of those ideas. It's not what material you are choosing as much as which skill you would like to start with.

Let's do the argue one but use fashion magazines.

Fine. Now that's your idea for school. What would you like your parents to do that might help you?

Nothing.

Wrong answer. They need to help in some way. You need more practice than just in school. We could do the same "argue with the author" technique at home but with a different magazine and you could compare your argument with your parents' points of view.

Students and parents often need specific ideas or a list from which to choose to come up with their suggestions.

We would never agree.

Agreeing isn't what it's about. Every reader is entitled to his or her personal thought about the issue, but you have to be able to back up your thoughts with reasons or nobody listens to you.

That one is probably not going to fly.

Okay, how about letting them help you with vocabulary flashcards? We'll make up some interesting words, and your job is to tell your parents what the word or phrase makes you think of, and they do the same for you. This is tying what you read to what you already know. Good readers do it all the time.

Fine.

Now you have a school and a home idea. We need one for you to do by yourself for practice.

Why can't I do the argue one by myself?

Good idea. We can have that idea in both your column and mine. We will practice at school and then you can do a passage for yourself.

Once Rhonda knows the procedure and is prepared for her role during the meeting, the teacher explains how growth will be measured and charted by the teacher, parents and by Rhonda herself.

Self-assessment has been shown by research to increase and maintain student motivation. It can start with the youngest students. It is critically important for the student to be given clear criteria and guidelines for evaluating and tracking their own progress. Rubrics, checklists, guided questions for journals, and "anchor papers" or samples of quality work and conferencing opportunities help accomplish this.

Referral Step 9

Now Rhonda and the team are ready for the meeting.

Once the DATA goal has been verified and or adjusted by the parents and students as being on target, the Baseline Data and Planning Form is given to all team members. This allows them to know enough about the case prior to the meeting to enable them to prepare intervention ideas that are a direct match to the goal and this particular student's style.

If the members feel the Baseline Form and work samples do not give enough information, they are free to contact the referring teacher and get the information they need before deciding upon the interventions for the problem-solving meeting.

The meeting process is the same for young children as older ones. After the student has been helped with developing the strategies she will present, the advocate often needs to help the student express these thoughts during the actual meeting. The advocate should give the student the **minimum** amount of support needed in order to get her to take an active part in the planning.

Don't Admire the Problem—Do Something!

What does the problem-solving meeting look like?

The problem-solving meeting agenda is basically:

Introductions, welcome, and focus on the DATA goal (what we hope to achieve)	3 min.
Brainstorm ideas for home, school, and student	9 min.
Select the plan of action	3 min.
Decide how to track progress at home and school	3 min.
Set next meeting–who and when	2 min.

Considerations for scheduling the meetings:

1. Designating a specific day and time for problem-solving meetings is a good way to reduce the number of conflicting meeting schedules.
2. Even though there is a designated day, scheduling must remain flexible enough to accommodate parents who cannot attend at the typical times.
3. Offering childcare and transportation may make attending possible for parents who could not otherwise come.
4. Meetings should only take 20–25 minutes, but occasionally parents want to talk to some of the team members about other issues. These other things should be discussed only *after* the problem-solving meeting ends.
5. With flexible team membership, multiple meetings can be going on simultaneously. The administrator is not always required for follow-up meetings.
6. Parents who cannot come to the school for a meeting can be part of the process via phone conference. When using phone conferencing it is wise to make the following arrangements:
   a. Ask the parent to choose a time when he/she is free to talk with minimal distractions.
   b. Limit the number of people for the phone-conference team (i.e., two adults and the student) talking to the parent.
   c. Prior to the meeting, send the parent a form stating the DATA goal and providing places to take notes. This form should be similar to the one you will be using at your location.
   d. Send home a copy of forms you will be using to track progress and any other print material that would be helpful.
   e. Make certain you know if a translator is needed for parents not fluent in English.

Rules of the Road for Problem-Solving Meetings

Following certain "Rules of the Road" for meetings will increase chances that the atmosphere will remain welcoming and safe for everyone. Each team creates its own appropriate rules, but the following ideas are keys to a positive atmosphere:

1. The focus will be totally on ideas to help the student reach the DATA goal. There can be no discussion of current or past problems until the meeting ends.
2. During the brainstorming of ideas, clarifying questions are good, and value judgments are bad. All ideas are recorded. If you do not like an idea, you are under no obligation to choose it as your part of the action plan.
3. We begin and end our meetings on time to respect the schedule of the team. If you are late just slip in quietly.
4. We will keep conversations focused on the timed agenda items and work within the time framework designed.
5. All team members bring their calendars to the meetings so we can schedule follow-up dates before people leave.
6. If people violate the above rules, we agree to respectfully call them on it.

A key aspect of the problem-solving meeting is to establish a productive working relationship among the members: the teacher(s), experts, the student, and the student's family or caregivers. This positive and respectful atmosphere must be established and maintained in order to make this process run smoothly.

Everyone comes to the meeting with three intervention ideas: one for each category of home, school, and the student.

If the pre-meeting referral conference steps have been skillfully carried out, everyone will know that the purpose of the meeting is to develop a plan to accomplish the DATA goal. All team members will know their roles and will come prepared to contribute at least three high quality ideas to help the student (one for home, one for school, and one for the student to do for himself). No one should feel threatened or on the spot at this meeting because only *solutions* will be discussed. The team will pool helpful ideas and select items for action and ways of tracking results during this 20–25 minute meeting.

Here is a suggested template for recording the brainstorming ideas:

Home Ideas	School Ideas	Student Ideas
1. Summarize TV show 2. Use insert note taking 3. Paraphrase vocabulary and draw a picture to match the word 4. Use a web to show main idea and detail of a TV show	1. Teach summarizing 2. Teach insert note taking 3. Stop and reflect strategy 4. Model "argue with the author" 5. Use SQ3R study style	1. Put down key words as she reads 2. Draw symbols that match the main key concepts as she reads 3. Practice "argue with the author" 4. Write questions before reading and check with a friend

Example:

The problem-solving meeting for Rhonda was held, and interventions were selected for implementation both at home and at school. Rhonda also had some personal interventions for which she was responsible.

Team membership adjusts to bring the people with the most expertise for each individual case to the table.

After working for five weeks, the team held the first **follow-up meeting.** Data was presented by parents, teachers, and Rhonda about how the plan was working. Since reading was improving, the team decided to continue with the current plan and tackle an additional issue from the Strengths and Concerns Form. An occupational therapist would be added to the team to help with Rhonda's penmanship problems.

At the second follow-up meeting, the data showed that things were still going well. It was decided that the next meeting would only require the reading specialist, Mr. Lummer, the parents, and Rhonda as the follow-up team.

Never do with seven people what could be accomplished with four.

Building this kind of flexible tailor-made team makes efficient use of available resource people. The rule of efficiency is "Never do with seven people what could be accomplished with four."

Follow-up Meetings:

That which gets measured, gets done.

One complaint of many teams is the lack of follow-through. A major cause for this is the lack of accountability built into the system. As the saying goes, "That which gets measured, gets done." This is a basic human reaction to "too much to do with too little time to do it." You hear students say, "Does this count?" and you know that if the answer is "No," the amount of energy put into the task is going to decrease unless the activity is something the students really want to do. It is no different in problem-solving with adults. Without a plan for specific follow-up, in which each person is asked to report on the results, the best intentions may or may not materialize as people get busy with other things.

The follow-up meetings might go something like this:

1. The teacher shows progress charts or work samples and discusses whether the interventions chosen are showing the level of success specified in the DATA goal.
2. The parents report their observations and say whether they think things are progressing or whether a new or adjusted plan is needed.
3. The student makes the same kind of report.
4. If needed, a new or altered plan is put into place by using some of the brainstormed ideas from the last set of minutes or by adding new ideas.
5. The team decides who is needed for the next follow-up meeting and when that meeting will be scheduled. They also decide what evidence of success each person will watch for and record.

Follow-up meetings are generally scheduled four to six weeks apart. This gives the plan enough time to be properly implemented without letting it go on too long if parts of the plan are not working. Often the follow-up team is a subgroup of the original team.

New members may be included in the group if another aspect of a DATA goal is to be added or the DATA goal changes. This process of meet and follow-up goes on until the student no longer requires team assistance or he graduates, whatever comes first.

The follow-up meeting agenda is typically as follows:

Welcome and focus on the DATA goal:	2 min.
Each person reports evidence of progress:	6 min.
The group uses the data to determine the next steps:	7 min.
If the plan has been successful: ○ Discontinue the case or ○ Add a new DATA goal	
If the plan has not been successful: ○ Does it need more time? ○ Do the action steps need to be changed? ○ Does the DATA goal need to be changed?	
How will we continue to monitor progress?	3 min.
When will we meet again?	2 min.

Family Involvement in the Problem-Solving Process

Admiring the problem is out: Solving the problem is in.

One thing that keeps the process positive and productive is the development of an intentional plan for making the family and the student an integral part of the system. So many times you hear teachers say, "The thing that annoys me is the fact that we're killing ourselves trying to solve these problems, and the kids and their families aren't taking their part of these responsibilities seriously. This is nuts!" It's easy to criticize parents and kids for not stepping up to the plate, but most schools have failed to build the kinds of support into the system that make active family involvement likely.

Many parents and teachers tend to be reluctant to involve students in the problem-solving meetings. It is my experience that given a positive and supportive atmosphere, it is not only safe but also wise to include even small children. These are perfect opportunities for adults to model efficient problem-solving. Students who feel a part of the team are more likely to understand the purpose of the changes. They are also more likely to feel a sense of commitment as they add their opinions to the team discussion and see possibilities for success increase. Research on self-monitoring also supports the fact that motivation and the sense of responsibility is increased when students track their own progress and report back to the team on a regular basis.

By adding the parents and students as active members in identifying the problem, designing an action plan, and monitoring the evidence of progress, the plan becomes a shared one between home and school. In my school this made a huge difference in the number of parents who chose to attend problem-solving meetings (growing from 20% to 83% within four years). Not only did parents attend more frequently, but the kind of interaction was much more positive and supportive.

Research supports the idea that parental participation with schools improves academic achievement of students **(Henderson & Mapp, 2002)**.

I'd rather have a root canal than go to another meeting:

I am often asked what to do when the parents just refuse to come. Some people say that it is harder than ever to get parents involved in their children's school. Parents are just too busy; there are more dysfunctional families; the number of teen parents is growing; many parents have been alienated since they were students themselves. Even though there is some validity to these statements, there are many schools that have turned a history of weak and even negative parental involvement into trusting and supportive partnerships.

The question of what to do when the parents don't show doesn't have a simple answer. In fact, my answer is usually the question, "What is preventing them from coming?" Here are the three most frequent responses from faculties:

1. *They just don't care.*
2. *They don't have time.*
3. *They are frustrated and just don't want to face the problem.*

When asked, parents give some of the following as reasons why they choose not to attend meetings and become involved at school:

- *Those teachers think they are so high and mighty just because they have a degree. They treat me like I'm stupid. The fact is they are the ones who are clueless about what makes my child tick.*
- *Oh sure, tell them what is really bothering me. What if I do and they take it out on my child?*
- *I have heard what is the matter with my child for six years running. I don't need to go to another meeting to be told that story again. It ruins my day.*
- *I hated that school when I went there. I'll be darned if I'm going there now.*
- *I don't have anyone to watch the little kids.*
- *Nobody told me about the meeting.* (In several cases this meant, "I cannot read and the school sent a note" or "I don't understand English very well.")
- *I don't have transportation.*
- *I cannot attend meetings during the workday.* This is especially difficult for parents who are hourly-wage workers and will be docked for taking time off.

These are the kinds of statements made at scout meetings and ball games. Often the polite version of those statements sounds like, "I don't believe I can make it during the day" or "Oh, did I miss that meeting?" Whether you are getting the straight story or the run-around version, the message is the same. The parents have no trust that the school intends to help their child. They think the school wants to place blame and shift the responsibility, and the school thinks the parents are doing the same.

The online Child Trends Data Bank summarizes the research as saying, "Students with parents who are involved in their school tend to have fewer behavioral problems and better academic performance, and they are more likely to complete secondary school" (2003). This partnership takes work and is worth building.

Parents who feel that their ideas are valued are more enthusiastic about being part of the team.

Many of the barriers to this collaborative partnership lie in the way parents and schools have thought of and treated each other in the past. Schools have seen parents mainly as fundraisers, volunteers, supervisors who should see that the homework assigned is actually done, and enforcers who back up school rules and discipline policies. These roles are not negative practices, but they tend to "use" parents more than they "involve" them.

Creating a different environment, one in which parents feel that what they have to say is valued and helpful, can allow an attitude of trust and cooperation to flourish. This does not happen overnight. It will take frequent and consistent actions to convey the message that "parents and other caregivers are welcome and honored here."

Ways to increase the possibility of parents attending meetings:

1. Parents are very likely to participate in meetings that they see as valuable for their child's learning. Be specific about what you intend to accomplish and how you and the parents can work together to make a difference.
2. Make certain all communications are sent in language the parents can easily read and interpret.
3. Focus on strengths and interests the child brings to the situation that will help move the process forward.
4. Explain that this is not the first time you have worked on this type of problem and that many students and their families have figured out ways to overcome and/or cope with the issues successfully.
5. Offer to have someone pick parents up if they need transportation to a meeting or event.
6. Offer childcare so the parent can relax and pay attention.
7. Acknowledge the value of what the parents have done so far to help their child.
8. It is a parent's job to protect, defend, and see that the very best education possible is provided for their child. Don't say anything that smacks of, "You must understand that there are sixty-eight other children in this class and I can't do this for your child and not do it for the rest." As heartless as it may sound on the surface, parents who are worried about their own child don't focus on other children or parents' needs. They are there to see that *their child* gets what he needs. The best thing you can do is to communicate that you want the same thing. The dilemma is to figure out ways that are achievable and satisfactory to both of you.

Use good listening and meeting facilitation skills to keep all members actively involved and positive. The more parents feel that their ideas are valued, the more enthusiastic they are likely to be as part of the team.

What if the parent does not show up?

Assume there is an excellent reason why they are not there, and go ahead and have the meeting. Call the parents after the meeting, and let them know what action plan was selected for school and student. Read the suggestions for "home" to them, and ask what they want you to write into the minutes as their part of the plan. Offer to send the options home to them if they do not want to make a decision right then. Most parents respond positively if the caller maintains a "we all want to help your child" attitude. If the parent does not respond positively this time, you have lost nothing but a few minutes of your time.

I choose from my category and you choose from yours. Not telling each other what to do creates plans that are more likely to happen.

After each team member has contributed intervention ideas, the person responsible for implementation selects from the appropriate list. For example, only the student may choose from the student category; only the parent chooses his/her part in the plan from the parent list. This prevents potential conflicts (i.e., if I place an intervention in your category that you think is inappropriate or unrealistic, you write it on the paper but simply do not choose it as your action step). This way people feel heard but do not have to commit to doing something they cannot or will not implement. It is amazing how respectful and positive the atmosphere is using this format.

Nine Steps at a Referral Conference:

Purpose	Steps for the coach and referring person: (details in Chapter 2)
Focus the action	1. Develop a list of concerns to be addressed. Select one academic issue and one behavior issue from the lists that, if changed, would have a positive impact on several of the other problems. List student strengths we can build on. (*Strengths and Concerns Form)*
Gather baseline data	2. Ask for a description of the key concerns (i.e., frequency, severity, location, examples, what triggers the behavior, partially successful and unsuccessful interventions already tried). (*Baseline and Planning form in Chapter 2*)
Analyze the problem	3. Unravel the key symptoms in order to find out what root causes might be responsible for making this problem so difficult to solve. *(This is the "Five Reasons Deep" process discussed in Chapter 2.)*
Establish a clear short-term target	4. Develop a DATA goal (a hypothesis about what results can be reasonably expected in less than six weeks if a new approach is tried.) Specific ways of measuring results are also developed.
Put together an expert team	5. Select a team of people who could effectively create an action plan to achieve this goal. *(Baseline and Planning form)*
Plan to make the parents feel comfortable about being an active member of the team.	6. Decide who will discuss the DATA goal and meeting process with the parents. (Typically the teacher is the person who calls). a. Schedule the meeting time with the parent/guardian. b. Explain the process and gather family insights about the appropriateness of the suggested DATA goal. c. Ask the parents to take an active part in this problem-solving procedure by coming to the meeting with specific suggestions for how home and school can help reach the DATA goal. d. Offer to assist the parents in developing suggestions if they are having a difficult time coming up with ideas for interventions.
Courtesy call	7. Decide who will make the follow-up call (24–48 hours after the initial call) to the family to see if there are unanswered questions, concerns or needs for further assistance in selecting their three intervention strategies to bring to the meeting. The follow-up caller is a different person than the original caller.
Plan to make the student comfortable about participating as a team member	8. Select the student advocate. This person explains the procedures to the student, checks for agreement and insights that might affect the DATA goal, and helps the student develop his/her three strategies for the meeting. (Often this is the referring teacher's role if the teacher/student relationship is positive). (*Record steps 1, 2, 4–8 on Baseline and Planning Form*)
Focus on specific types of interventions	9. Distribute the Baseline and Planning Form and any work samples to the selected team members. This allows clarifying discussions to take place with the teacher, if needed.

Summary:

We need to change the way we serve *any* student who struggles in school and it doesn't need to be about labels. It will take more than simply changing testing guidelines, scheduling and meeting procedures to do this. It will take a change in **attitude and focus.**

The **attitude** must move from "learning and behavior problems are somebody else's job" to "educators, parents and resource people will work as a team to help each struggling student, regardless of label or lack of it."

The change in **focus** is from "what label to put on this student" to "what services and interventions will help this learner achieve maximum growth?" It will take a serious effort to change the way we do business and impact the lives of our students. If the results we are seeing are not more effective learning and better behavior for every type of student, then we are doing things the wrong way. If the data doesn't verify that our interventions are working we must *change the plan,* not just change the student label or placement.

Chapter Two

"If You Don't Know Where You're Going, You May End Up Someplace Else."

Yogi Berra

What the Referral Coach Needs to Know and Do

In this chapter we will look at the roles and responsibilities of referral coaches as they work through the nine steps that prepare the team members for the formal problem-solving meeting. There are basically three phases to this process:

Phase 1: Figuring out the root cause of the student's problem (Steps 1–3).
Phase 2: Setting a clear goal that will guide the intervention process (Step 4).
Phase 3: Selecting the team and making certain every member knows how to prepare to contribute to a productive meeting (Steps 5–9).

Chelsea: Ryan, I've been considering volunteering to be a referral coach. May I talk to you so I know just what I'm getting myself into?

Ryan: Sure.

Chelsea: What inspired you to become a coach?

Ryan: I suppose most of us had the same reason. We thought the training on problem-solving skills and designing interventions would serve us well in our own classrooms as well as enable us to help other teachers in the school.

It takes as much time and energy to work on the wrong problem as the right one.

Chelsea: And has it worked like that?

Ryan: Absolutely. In fact, I find myself using the skills as much in other areas of my life as I do at school. This process is a very different way of thinking though. It's a real mind-bender at first.

Chelsea: What do you mean?

Ryan: Teachers tend to be problem-solvers. We want to jump right in there and come up with a quick fix.

Chelsea: What's wrong with that?

Ryan: As a coach your job is to resist going to solutions until you are confident that you have identified the root cause of the problem. It takes as much time and energy to work on the wrong problem as the right one, so taking the time to do the analysis pays off. Our job is to avoid putting lots of energy into the wrong issues.

Chelsea: Okay. So what does a good referral session look like from start to finish?

The Referral Conference Checklist:

Steps: The referring person (typically the teacher) gathers basic information (work samples, cum folder data that is germane to the case, etc.)

The coach then helps the referring person:

1. Develop a list of both **academic and behavioral concerns.** Choose just one academic and one behavioral issue to start with.
2. Collect the **baseline data** that serves as a reference point to help judge the effectiveness of all interventions and assessments. (The coach may need to assist the referring person in identifying and gathering this data if it is not already available.)
3. Use the "Five Reasons Deep" analysis to **identify the root cause** of the problem.
4. Set a clear and specific **DATA goal** to guide the rest of the process.
5. Decide if a formal problem-solving meeting is needed to generate intervention options. If yes, the coach assists the teacher in **selecting the right time, place, and people** to help. The coach may or may not go on to serve as a member of this team. If no formal meeting is to be scheduled, the coach helps the teacher create an action and monitoring plan.
6. Decide **who will work with the parents** to make certain they are comfortable with their roles as involved team members.
7. Decide **who will make the courtesy call** to see that the family is prepared for the meeting and has all immediate questions and concerns addressed before the meeting.
8. Decide **who will take on the role of student advocate** to make certain the student is ready to assume an active part in the problem-solving process.
9. **Distribute Baseline and Planning form and work samples** to all team members so they can come prepared with targeted interventions.

Advantages of the referral process:

- Referrers have a trained sounding-board to help them verbalize and analyze what they know about a student.
- Prevents the wheel-spinning caused by working on symptoms instead of root causes.
- Gets help more quickly for students who are in need of interventions and accommodations.
- More powerful and effective interventions are designed because the focus is on a specific and a defined target goal.
- Involves the student and family as true partners with the school in problem-solving.

Disadvantages of using the referral process:

- Requires more time to prepare for the meeting.
- Difficulty of learning new skills of diagnosis and prescribing.
- Resistance to changing traditional ways of operating.
- The attitude of "Just test him and dispatch him, he's not my problem" dies hard.

Nitty-Gritty Questions About the Coaching Process:

1. **Who should be a coach?**

   Many times schools start out using administrators, psychologists, and counselors as coaches. They then add special education teachers and general education teachers who show an interest in learning the coaching skills. In an ideal world, every person on the staff would become proficient at using the coaching skills. It's just a good way for everyone to think about problem-solving.

2. **Why would you use more than one coach in a referral session?**

   When a coach is just beginning, it is often easier to have a partner who can help ask the right questions and process the teacher's answers. Even an experienced coach may find that being assisted by people who have specialized training in the area of concern is helpful (i.e., a coach who is not a reading expert but knows that reading is the prime area of concern may want to invite a reading expert to assist at the referral conference).

3. **What can the referring teacher do to make the process go faster?**

   Gather the following types of information **before** the referral meeting:

   a. Attendance, medical and any previous referral information
   b. Work samples, diagnostic test results, and observation data collected
   c. List of interventions that showed signs of promise and others known not to get a positive response for this student
   d. List of times parents were contacted and interventions cooperatively tried
   e. Past teachers' observations and grades
   f. Notes from conferences held with student before this referral

4. **What do you do when the referring teacher wants the student tested but really thinks he might just be lazy?**

   Many times students seen as lazy do, in fact, have a true disability. The frustration these students face daily can result in a depressed and hopeless attitude. Testing might eventually be appropriate.

   By the same token, many students walking around with IEPs do not have a disability at all; they just need an extra boost. The only way faculty members think extra help is possible is to provide an IEP. Fortunately, we are now able to provide services without labeling students who do not require intensive and long-term assistance. Federal guidelines allow for fifteen percent of the special education budget to be used as prevention to keep students from falling into the cycle of failure.

A coach needs to be ready to explain how a solid intervention and monitoring process can get the appropriate help without unnecessary delays and labeling. This process is known as RtI (Response to Intervention). If the student needs an IEP, this process will not only provide immediate assistance while the more involved MFE process occurs, but will also serve as part of the required data for the MFE. This can be a win-win situation for everyone.

How in the world do you get time to do the coaching?

Ideas for creating time to be a referral coach:

1. Train enough coaches so the entire burden is not shouldered by a small group of people.
2. Incorporate regular coaching periods into the coach's schedule.
3. Pair coaches so they can combine classes occasionally to release one partner for some coaching responsibilities. Assign an aide or parent volunteer to assist with these double-class lessons.
4. Coaching time replaces hall, bus, cafeteria, study hall duties, etc.
5. Floating substitutes release coaches and the teachers they need to meet with.
6. Extended contracts for referral coaching responsibilities. (This option should be used with care. Districts where supplementary contracts are awarded on a tenure basis can be a blessing or a disaster depending upon the individuals you end up with. This option also tends to work against the concept of eventually expanding the coaching pool to include as many faculty experts as possible.)
7. Have aides, partner-teachers, etc., supervise students during activities such as assemblies, on-line practice lessons, and other study or work times that can be done without the teacher's presence.
8. Create regular times (beyond the student contact day) when coaching and other types of planning meetings can be scheduled.
9. Plan times for the problem-solving experts to update the coaches on the newest research for solving student academic and behavior problems.

Coaching Process

It is critical that the referring teacher feels comfortable, supported, and listened to throughout the process. If the teacher feels like the coach is the "referral Gestapo," the process is guaranteed to be unproductive.

If the teacher feels like the coach is the "referral Gestapo," the process is guaranteed to be unproductive.

Start out the referral conference by asking the teacher to list all the academic and behavioral symptoms that are a source of concern for this student. Use paraphrasing and probing questions as active listening tools to encourage the teacher to *specifically* describe the student's strengths and key areas of concern. Get as clear a picture as possible before selecting the high-impact area as the beginning focus point for this student.

Step 1: Identifying Strengths and Concerns

Strengths and Concerns Interview	
Academic Concerns:	**Behavior Concerns:**
Strengths to build on:	

Here's is a sample of how these conversations often go:

Sylvia: *Hi, Dante. Who are we going to talk about today?*

Dante: *Anita is my student of the hour.*

Sylvia: *Go ahead, give me a list of both academic and behavioral concerns for Anita. I'll use this interview sheet to organize our thoughts.*

Dante: *Okay. Academically Anita is about two years behind in both reading and math. Since her reading is so poor, it is affecting every other subject, because in fourth grade she needs to read the texts by herself.*

During the Strengths/Concern part of the referral conference, if the concerns are too general, a coach's job is to ask for a more specific description (i.e., "What exactly do you see that makes you think she's ADHD?" or "What does he do that makes you say he's immature?")

Sometimes the coach needs to offer assistance in gathering data.

Sylvia: *What makes Anita's reading so poor? Is it beginning and ending sounds, blending sounds, basic sight vocabulary, summarizing . . .*

Dante: *She has those first grade skills, but to tell you the truth I'd have to go back and check to see which exact skills are secure.*

Sylvia: *Do you want to check on those, or do you want the Title I Reading teacher to give a quick survey for you?*

Dante: *Yes, a quick assessment would help. I think reading is a big part of her math problem, too. She's okay with computation, but word problems kill her.*

Sylvia: *That reading issue spills over every time. What behavior concerns do you have?*

Make certain the teacher is thinking beyond discipline problems when you ask for behavior concerns.

Dante: *She is no behavior problem. In fact you hardly know she's there, which leads to another major concern. Many times she's* ***not*** *there. She's missed about five days, and it's only November. I don't know what the deal is with that mother. She writes an illness excuse, but I hear Anita saying that they oversleep and her mother just writes the day off. She cannot afford days off.*

Sylvia: *I'll make a note to double-check where the office is on that one. When I asked about behaviors, I didn't mean to imply just discipline problems. Are there any social, emotional, or work habit issues that affect her learning?*

Dante: *She has a hard time concentrating. She is on the shy side, but she does have friends. She doesn't ask for help when she is confused. Are those the kinds of things you are looking for?*

Sylvia: *Exactly. Here's a list that might trigger a few more ideas for both strengths and weaknesses. See what you think.*

List of Strengths to get you started

Communication:
Asks questions
Sees relationships
Memorizes well
Expresses feelings openly
Believes in himself
Excited about learning
Writes well
Draws well
Is a reflective thinker
Organized
Does things step-by-step
High energy
Creative thinker
Works well alone
Likes to solve problems
Good with three-dimensional tasks
Handles setbacks well
Works within deadlines
Likes competition
Sees many options and solutions
Works hard
Wants to succeed

Reading
Uses parts of book (index, glossary . . .)
Can blend sounds
Uses vowel rules to sound out words
Can identify sight words
Attends to punctuation when reading
Can identify main idea
Can separate important from unimportant
Visualizes as he reads
Links text to prior knowledge
Enjoys reading

Math strengths:
Recognizes numerals
One to one correspondence
Counts well
Understands place value
Understands regrouping
Understands equal
Can visualize the problem
Understands math vocabulary
Can solve multiple ways
Can explain his reasoning

Memory
Recalls details seen
Recalls details done
Recalls feelings
Puts things in order
Recalls after practice
Can link new ideas to old
Remembers the next day
Remembers a week later
Strong long-term memory
Visualizes to remember
Develops memory tricks

Interests:
Sports
Animals
Art, music
Computers
Writing
Collections
Cars, bikes . . .
Fashion

How do we decide where to start?

Focus is the key. Going for small, powerful successes is much more efficient than diluting energy by trying to solve all the problems at once.

Sylvia: Now I would like you to pick two concerns to serve as starting points for Anita; one issue from the academic and one from the behavior list.

Dante: But how can I just pick one? She has to get going on several, or she's going to get further and further behind.

Sylvia: A ***laser-like focus*** *on just a few things will get us further in the long run. You won't just ignore the other issues, but I will help you focus on priorities. Choose two items that are most likely to have a positive domino effect on other issues. That will allow us to get more done with less effort.*

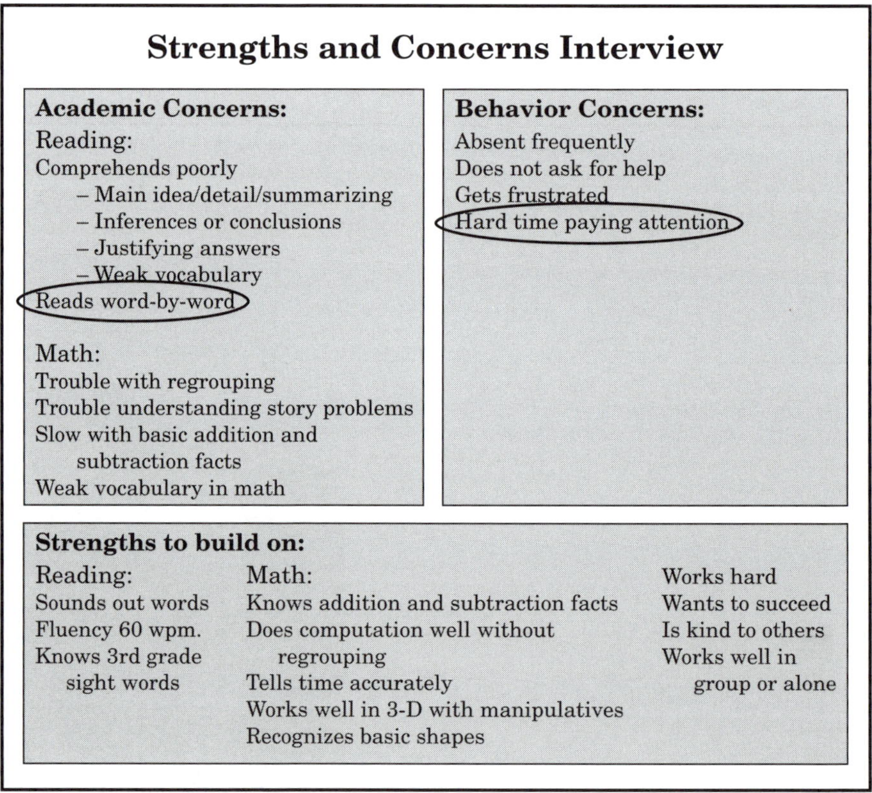

Strengths and Concerns Interview

Academic Concerns:
Reading:
Comprehends poorly
– Main idea/detail/summarizing
– Inferences or conclusions
– Justifying answers
– Weak vocabulary
Reads word-by-word

Math:
Trouble with regrouping
Trouble understanding story problems
Slow with basic addition and subtraction facts
Weak vocabulary in math

Behavior Concerns:
Absent frequently
Does not ask for help
Gets frustrated
Hard time paying attention

Strengths to build on:

Reading:
Sounds out words
Fluency 60 wpm.
Knows 3rd grade sight words

Math:
Knows addition and subtraction facts
Does computation well without regrouping
Tells time accurately
Works well in 3-D with manipulatives
Recognizes basic shapes

Works hard
Wants to succeed
Is kind to others
Works well in group or alone

Ask the teacher to limit the scope, with the promise to pick up other issues once progress is seen with the first set of goals. As a starting point, guide the teacher to select the highest leverage issues that, when changed, will have a positive impact on other concerns on the list. After selecting the focus issues, list baseline information for these key items.

Step 2: Identifying Baseline Data

Baseline Data and Planning Form

Student Name *Anita Billis* Date referred *11/13* Referring person(s) *Mr. Villa*

Steps 1 & 2 - Key issues to be addressed*: *Fluency in reading and Attention span*

Step 3 - Baseline data:**

Frequency: *Reads 53 words per minute, 5 of 52 days absent, 100% errors on word problems*

Severity: *Presently averaging "D" in math and reading, science and social studies*
Attends for an average of 7 min. if actively involved; about 6 min. if just listening

Places problem is observed: *Affecting all content subjects, Not fine arts*

Times when problem is observed: *All times when reading is involved*

Things that trigger the problem: *Reading assignments or math problems involving reading*
Attention is much worse if task is complex.

Strategies that resulted in positive response: *Buddy reading, oral responses, visual cues and listening to books on tape*

Strategies found to be ineffective: *Large group instruction, independent reading*

Reinforcements found to be effective: *Stickers, praise, home contact*

Reinforcements not recommended: *Extra time to do the work, staying in for recess*

Step 4 - DATA Goal*****:**

Step 5 - Team members:

Step 6 - Who will contact parents?

Step 7 - Who will make the follow-up call?

Step 8 - Who will prepare the student?

Referral taken by ___________________

*Attach Strengths and Concerns form ** Attach work samples and observation data *** See "Five Reasons" document

Step 3: Managing Coaching Conversations—"Five Reasons Deep Analysis"

This is perhaps the most difficult skill and, along with the setting of the DATA goals, the most essential part of the problem-solving process. Identifying root causes is difficult because most teachers are trained to diagnose skill needs rather than root causes. If the process were as simple as figuring out what skills were needed, most teachers would have resolved the problems quickly. Students who are being referred generally have had the same instruction as other kids, but for some reason (root cause) typical instructional strategies alone do not work for them. The key to identifying root causes is looking beyond what typically works to see what it is that makes this student's way of learning different. Once we uncover that, the interventions that are likely to be effective become more obvious, and we will waste less time trying things that are ineffective.

Helpful questions to ask yourself as you conduct a "Five Reasons Deep" discussion:

1. Is the issue within our circle of influence (things we can change)?
2. Is the teacher's response too general or too specific to be clear about the possible root cause of the problem?
3. Are we jumping to solutions before root causes have been identified?
4. Is my next "five reasons deep" question based on the key concept just mentioned by the teacher?
5. Does my question ask for clarification or analysis?

1. Staying within the circle of influence:

Coaches need to avoid letting the conversation drift into the blaming mode or into belaboring things over which you have no control. If "out of our circle of influence" talk isn't short circuited, the discussion ends up admiring the problem and causing feelings of helplessness—not a good mental place for problem-solving! The coach needs to watch for these types of statements and redirect the conversation to issues we *can* control or at least influence.

Words that lead to "out of your circle" conversations: he is immature, she has a low IQ, parents just don't care, family is going through a divorce, he moves a lot, she's autistic, dad does drugs, he has a brother just like that, the administration never backs us, last year's teacher did a bad job, next year they won't make any accommodations, the state test is impossible because . . .

2. Talk is too specific or too general:

Avoid talking in vague generalities like: he is lazy, she just doesn't care, she has a low IQ, he is disrespectful. Ask for specific behaviors so you as the coach know you are talking about the same problem. Clarifying questions can get you back on track with your analysis. Example:

Teacher: He is disrespectful.

Coach: Tell me what he does that makes you think that.

Dwelling on incidents that are too specific is just as non-productive as being too general. The coach may have to ask questions or use paraphrasing to take the conversation up a notch to see what specific pattern the teacher sees. Example:

Teacher: Yesterday he told the music teacher that he didn't have to if he didn't want to. Then on Friday he. . . .

Coach: So are you're saying that he is consistently sassy, or is it more that he is argumentative?

3. We're jumping to solutions too early:

Know what your problem is before you try to solve it.

Coaches need to avoid jumping into problem-solving before figuring out what the root problem is. Working on the symptoms or the wrong problems is a waste of precious time. Example:

Teacher: Jerry is failing in science.

Coach should ask: ***Why*** *is Jerry failing?*

Coach should not ask: What have you tried so far? This type of question leads to premature solutions.

4. Keeping the conversation focused:

Coaches only offer alternatives when the teacher gets stuck.

Link your question to the key word in the answer the teacher just gave. This keeps the analysis from going all over the place and stops the coach from thinking for the teacher.

Teacher: Darlene is constantly ***disrupting*** *the class.*

Coach should ask: Why do you think she ***disrupts****?*

Coach should not say: Do you think she's bored? This has the coach doing the analysis instead of the teacher. The coach only offers alternatives when the teacher gets stuck.

5. Are we going deep or wide?

It may take more than five questions to get to the root cause.

Clarifying questions are for the Strengths and Concerns interview. Coaches need to stick to analysis questions during the "Five Reasons" interview.

The premise behind "Five Reasons Deep" is that it takes at least five good analysis questions to get to a root cause. More times than not, it will take more than five questions. Recognizing the difference between a clarifying question that merely asks for a description and an analysis question that asks for a reason is critical to identifying the root cause. Starting analysis questions with the word "why" is generally a safe bet, but there are alternatives.

Variations on analysis questions that start with the word "why" are:

"What do you think could be causing that?"
"What could be influencing his decisions to do that?"
"What is interfering with her ability to . . . "
"What is keeping him from improving?"

Questions to refocus "out of the circle of influence" talk:

"What other reasons could there be for that problem?"
"What is a cause we have some ability to change?"

When a teacher gets stuck, the coach may need to give two or three possible root causes for the behavior or problem.

"Some students who cannot pay attention have a difficult time *processing things visually* while others cannot identify things *taught in auditory ways*. Other students might just be overwhelmed by the volume of material coming at them. Do any of those sound like possibilities for this student?"

Getting a teacher unstuck when a "why" question results in an "I have no idea" answer is a key skill for the coaching process. The more possibilities for root causes the coach knows (see examples in Chapter 4), the easier it will be to assist the teacher in drilling down to the core issue. Once the root cause is identified, a clear and specific DATA goal can be set and the problem-solving process becomes productive and focused.

Let's Practice The Five Whys:

The following are actual examples that are typical of some new coaches' efforts to conduct "Five Reasons" analyses conversations. Even though the process is called "Five Reasons Deep," there are times it works in only four questions and other times when it could take fourteen questions to get to a root cause. For practice purposes, the entire "Five Reasons" conversation is not necessarily included in each of these examples.

Use the checklist to evaluate these "Five Reasons Deep" analyses. Identify the coach errors and see if you can reword the question to fix it.

"Five Reasons Deep" mental checklist:

1. Is this something we can change?
2. Is the teacher's response too general or too specific to follow with an analysis question?
3. Are we jumping to solutions?
4. Is my question based on the most important concept in the answer before it?
5. Does my question ask for reasons "why" or just clarification?

Case 1. Kisha doesn't get her work done.

Coach says:	Teacher says:
1. Why isn't Kisha finishing her work?	1. She distracts others and just doesn't do it.
2. How is she distracting others?	2. She won't stay where she is supposed to be.
3. So what do you do when she roams around?	3. I make her stay in for recess or write a note to the mom.
4. Are you sure she is capable of the work?	4. Yes.

What problems do you see with this coach's questions?

How would you fix the problem(s)?

Let's analyze what you just read.

These alternative questions are only suggestions and may not be the exact ones you decided to write. There may be several logical responses to these cases but all good responses do have to be variations on the question "**why** does this child do this or think this way?"

Case 1. Kisha

The first question asked by the coach was fine.

Because the teacher does not exactly answer the question of *why* Kisha doesn't finish the work, the coach assumed, "she's busy causing distractions so work does not get done" as the implied answer. If this is correct, the second question asked should have been "Why do you think she chooses to distract rather than do her work?" Instead, the coach asked a clarifying question about distractions. It is okay to ask a clarifying question if the teacher is being too vague and you need specifics, but this was not one of those cases. The coach needed to direct the conversation back to the original problem.

The third coach question is leading the teacher to discuss interventions. This is never done during the "Five Reasons" analysis part of the referral. The question should have been, "*What causes her to* want to move around so much?"

The fourth coach question led the conversation in a totally new direction. The coaches should avoid doing this. The teacher needs to be the analyzer, and the coach is the listener and questioner until the teacher gets stuck. This coach took the lead from the teacher.

Case 1. Kisha doesn't get her work done (one possible revision).

Coach says:	Teacher says:
1. Why isn't Kisha finishing her work?	1. She distracts others and just doesn't do it.
2. Why is she choosing to distract them instead of doing her work?	2. I think she gets frustrated.
3. Why do you think she is frustrated?	3. The work is just too hard for her.
4. What about the work makes it too hard?	4. Her reading and writing are way below level.
5. What causes the reading to be so far below level?	5. Her phonics skills are fine but she reads so slowly she cannot remember what she reads.
6. Why do you think she reads so slowly?	6. I think she hasn't learned to read in phrases yet.
* So are you saying that fluency is where we need to start?	* Yes. That and basic vocabulary.

* Sometimes it takes more than just five reasons to get to a root cause. If you need to ask a clarifying question, do not count it as a numbered analysis question.

Let's Practice

"Five Reasons Deep" mental checklist:

1. Is this something we can change?
2. Is the teacher's response too general or too specific?
3. Are we jumping to solutions?
4. Is my question based on the most important concept?
5. Does my question ask for reasons "why"?

Case 2. Andy doesn't know his letters and sounds

Coach says:	Teacher says:
1. What is keeping Andy from learning the letters and sounds?	1. He just cannot remember them.
2. How are his writing skills?	2. They stink unless I am right next to him. His invented spelling is not even in the ballpark when he works by himself.
3. How are Andy's social skills?	3. Fine. He has lots of friends and he is polite and cooperative.

What problems do you see with this coach's questions?

How would you fix the problem(s)?

Let's analyze what you just read.

Case 2. Andy

The first question was fine, but the second changed the topic completely and the third changed the subject again. This coach seems not to understand the purpose of digging down to a root cause as opposed to interviewing the teacher as you do in the strengths and concerns interview.

Case 2. Andy doesn't know his letters and sounds (one possible revision).

Coach says:	Teacher says:
1. What is keeping Andy from learning the letters and sounds?	1. He just cannot remember them.
2. What is interfering with his memory?	2. I really don't know.
3. Sometimes kids need more practice or a different kind of practice. Sometimes they cannot hear sounds or if they can hear them they cannot discriminate one from another. Do any of these sound right?	3. I don't think Andy can tell one sound from another. Rhyming words just don't click for him. Clapping patterns don't either.
* So holding auditory things in his memory might be a difficulty. We could check that out as a possible cause.	* I think that is a good place to start.
4. If that hypothesis doesn't check out, is there anything else that could be causing this?	4. Maybe he just needs more practice.
* Is it more practice or a different kind of practice?	* I suppose a different kind is what I really meant. What we have been doing is certainly not working.

* A needed clarifying question, not numbered as a part of the analysis.

In this case the coach had a list of possible root causes in her head, and when the teacher got stuck on question two, the coach was able to offer some possibilities for consideration.

The coach and teacher need to validate their suspicions of auditory memory as a potential root cause by asking for a quick screening.

Let's Practice

The following is a good coaching conversation. See if you can figure out what the coach is doing that makes it effective.

Any line labeled "*" is the teacher's code for a clarifying pause in the analysis.

"Five Reasons Deep" mental checklist:

1. Is this something we can change?
2. Is the teacher's response too general or too specific?
3. Are we jumping to solutions?
4. Is my question based on the most important concept?
5. Does my question ask for reasons "why"?

Case 3. Jerome's math skills are three levels below grade level.

Coach says:	Teacher replies:
1. What is keeping Jerome from doing well in *math?*	1. He doesn't always follow the math *procedures* accurately.
2. Why do you think he cannot follow the math *procedures?*	2. I'm really not sure. He might be *ADHD.*
3. Many *ADHD* kids do follow math procedures. What other reason might there be?	3. He might just be *lazy.*
* Tell me what he does that makes you think that *laziness* is the problem.	* He doesn't bother to stop and think. He just guesses and goes. What do you think we can do about that?
* Let's make sure we both understand what's causing the problem, then we'll try to brainstorm some solutions.	* That's fine.
4. So why do you think he doesn't bother to stop and think?	4. I really don't know. That's why I'm here talking to you.
5. Could it be that he doesn't care about getting answers wrong, or is it that he is impulsive, or could it be a lack of attention to detail?	5. Gee, that's a pretty good list. How about all of the above? Actually, I think he wants to do well but just can't *slow himself down* enough to attend to the details.
* So you think that if we could just teach Jerome to *slow down* and pay attention to details, his math problem would solve itself?	* I'm not sure that's the whole answer, but I think it is a good starting place.

Let's analyze what you just read.

Case 3. Jerome

Coach question 1 was right on because it asks the teacher to make an educated guess as to what is causing the math problem.

Coach question 2 was also appropriate, because it used the words "math procedures" from the teacher's answer to go one level deeper into the cause.

Coach response 3 accomplished two things. It redirected the teacher from an "out of his circle of influence," since disabilities are not under our control. It also refocused the teacher back to the response, which stated that math procedures were the source of the problem.

In the first * question, the coach chose not to ask an analysis question because clarification of the term "lazy" was necessary before moving on. This moved the conversation from a vague generalization down to a more productive level.

The second * was not designed to be an analysis question either. The coach had to keep the teacher from jumping into a discussion about interventions too early.

Coach response 4 asks the teacher to analyze why Jerome doesn't stop and think, which is a rephrase of the teacher's response from the first * question.

Coach's response 5 is an effort to get the teacher unstuck. Once a teacher says any form of "I have no idea," that is a signal for the coach to offer a few root cause alternatives. A coach must have some knowledge of what might cause such behavior or both the teacher and the coach are stuck. This is where knowledge of the research is of vital importance.

The last * is the coach's effort to double check for understanding of what the teacher is saying through paraphrasing or summarizing. This helps both the coach and the teacher rethink what conclusion they are drawing and clarify any possible miscommunication before writing a DATA goal.

Let's Practice

Use the checklist below to evaluate these "Five Reasons Deep" analyses. Identify the coach errors and see if you can reword the question to fix it.

"Five Reasons Deep" mental checklist:

1. Is this something we can change?
2. Is the teacher's response too general or too specific?
3. Are we jumping to solutions?
4. Is my question based on the most important concept?
5. Does my question ask for reasons "why"?

Case 4. Aaron refuses to do his work.

Coach says:	Teacher says:
1. Why is Aaron refusing to work?	1. He's bored.
2. What do you think is causing the boredom?	2. I think he's just a rebel. His home life is an absolute mess.
3. What causes his home life to be such a mess?	3. He bounces back and forth from his mom's house to his dad's. He also has low self-esteem.
4. Do you think he just wants your attention?	4. Yes. He feels comfortable with me.

What problems do you see with this coach's questions?

How would you fix the problem(s)?

Let's analyze what you just read.

Case 4. Aaron

This coach was doing fine with the first two questions. Both were directly based upon the key words from the teacher responses, and both were analysis questions designed to get the teacher to think more deeply.

The third coach question invited the teacher to analyze an "out of his circle of influence" issue. We cannot control the home life, so that should not be a topic of discussion even though it is, in fact, an influencing issue. The coach should have acknowledged the fact that the home life would make things harder for Aaron and then refocused the teacher on a controllable issue. "I know Aaron has a difficult home situation, but since we cannot control that, let's talk about another reason he might be acting like a rebel in your room instead of doing his work."

The last coach question was not based upon any response originated by the teacher. The coach needs to keep the focus on why Aaron is not doing his work.

Case 4. Aaron refuses to do his work (possible revision).

Coach says:	Teacher says;
1. Why is Aaron refusing to work?	1. He's bored.
2. What do you think is causing the boredom?	2. I think he's just a rebel.
3. Why would being a rebel cause him to choose not to work?	3. I think he is angry with the world.
* So he is angry with you and refuses to be cooperative?	* No, he and I are fine. His home life is what makes him angry. It's a mess and he is caught in the middle.
4. I know Aaron has a difficult home situation but since we cannot control that, what is another reason he might be refusing to work?	4. Well, he is very frustrated and so his concentration is awful.
5. So what causes this frustration?	5. I think he is so worried about what is happening at home that he cannot keep his mind on his school work.
* That makes sense. So are you saying that if we work on helping him cope with those worries he will be able to apply himself, or is it more than that?	* I really do think that is the key issue. He wants to do well and is very capable but he just cannot cope with the stress. That's where I would like to begin.

The family situation is out of our circle of influence, but we can attempt to support a student who is dealing with stress. These children can be taught coping and relaxation skills that will not solve their problems but will give them some tools to deal with difficult situations and their ability to concentrate.

Let's Practice

Case 5: Robin is crying in class

Coach says:	Teacher says:
1. Why do you think Robin cries in class? 2. Why isn't she getting her writing done? 3. Why do you think she's crying over it when in previous years she was fine? 4. Do you think that is because she prefers to have a male teacher?	1. She isn't getting her writing done. 2. She's not retaining the information. 3. She says school is stupid except for Mr. Wagnor's class. 4. I don't know.

What problems do you see with this coach's questions?

How would you fix the problem(s)?

Case 5. Robin

The first two coach questions are on target, launching from the teacher's own words "crying" and "getting her writing done."

The third question ignores the teacher's statement about retaining information. The question, "What do you think is keeping her from retaining information" has a better likelihood of identifying what is different about the way Robin learns. The question about what is different this year may be a question that could help but would be better asked after pursuing the line of thought started by the teacher.

Case 5. Robin is crying in class (possible revision)

Coach says:	Teacher says:
1. Why do you think Robin cries in class?	1. She isn't getting her writing done.
2. Why isn't she getting her writing done?	2. She's not retaining the information.
3. What is preventing her from retaining information?	3. Well, she takes lousy notes in class for one thing.
4. What keeps her from taking better notes?	4. I don't know. We have practiced different types of note taking but she really messes it up.
5. Do you think she cannot sort through the information to focus on what is important, or could it be she cannot organize herself, or is she disconnecting because she needs more of a challenge?	5. The challenge isn't it. Her organization is poor and maybe she can't sort through the details.
6. Let's go a bit deeper on the organization. Why do you think she has such a hard time organizing?	6. It seems like she cannot put things or ideas into categories. She doesn't know where to start, and she doesn't sequence things well.
* So are you saying that if we teach her to categorize and sequence things, her problems would be reduced?	* Yes, that's a great place to start. Then I think we will still have to go back and work on main idea and details, but that is really categorizing, isn't it? That should work.

Step 4: Developing DATA Goals.

D — **What adults do Differently**
A — **What the student will Achieve**
T — **In what amount of Time**
A — **as Assessed by . . .**

Coaches help teachers convert the conclusions from the "Five Reasons Deep" process into achievement and behavioral DATA goals that go beyond accommodations to interventions. These goals generally use the sentence starter, "If we teach (*the student*) to (*target behavior*) . . ." Teaching a new skill, a coping skill, or replacing unproductive behavior with a productive behavior is what the adults will ***do Differently.*** Using the sentence starter to write the DATA goal is more likely to result in an intervention plan as opposed to simply an accommodation plan (crutch).

Accommodations are aids that help minimize the damage of a problem situation or disability.

The DATA goal needs to identify an intervention plan rather than simply an accommodation plan. Accommodations are aids that help minimize the damage of a problem situation or disability. Interventions are the treatments that make the student more self-sufficient.

Examples of accommodations:

A **crutch and cast** help protect the leg from further damage while therapy and healing take place.

A **buddy to read with** reduces the chance of missing concepts in science due to inability to read the required text.

Both the crutch and the reading buddy are accommodations that fix nothing but are helpful as long as the teacher or student doesn't think of them as the ultimate goal.

Many students have accommodation plans without the companion interventions designed to get rid of or reduce dependence on the accommodations. These students are at risk of ending up with what we term *LEARNED HELPLESSNESS.*

You can recognize an ACCOMMODATION by the fact that someone other than the learner is doing most of the work and thinking (i.e., I shorten assignments, provide a template, or dole out rewards for work . . .). When I stop doing these things you may be right back where you started—dependent on someone else.

Interventions are the treatments that make the student more self-sufficient.

INTERVENTIONS change the way the student thinks about solving his own problems. Once an intervention works, the student will be able to cope with or do things on his own even if a support person is not available (i.e., I teach you to break your own assignments into shorter pieces, use a graphic organizer to visualize relationships, or teach you to self-assess your own work).

D The critical word is **Differently.** As Einstein said, "Doing the same thing and expecting a new result is the definition of insanity." We often make the insane decision to do more of what we have already tried, just louder and slower or in a new place.

Remember, if it looks like the teacher will work harder than the student in this goal, the teacher will learn more.

As we develop this DATA goal, one question a coach asks is, "Have we tried this already?" If the answer is yes, the next question is, "In what ways will our approach be different this time?" The second question is, "Is this plan an intervention or simply an accommodation?" It needs to be a clear intervention idea but not a specific approach (i.e., Teach Sam to use graphic organizers rather than teach him to use a Venn diagram. Teach Mary to self-assess, rather than teach Mary to use the writing checklist).

Broader "Do Differently" statements enable the team to brainstorm a variety of ways to achieve the desired results.

A What change will the student ***Achieve*** in relation to the teacher's original concern. "Jill will increase her ability to sit still" is a student goal that is useful in the school setting but has limited value in real life. "Lamar will be able to extend his attention" targets a skill that will serve Lamar well throughout his life.

T The ***Time frame*** needs to be between two to six weeks. Letting an intervention go longer than six weeks without reviewing its effects is asking for trouble. There needs to be some positive sign that this intervention is getting results or the team should consider the possibility that some adjustment needs to be made. The adjustment could be a tweak to the original idea, an entirely new strategy, or a rethinking of the original DATA goal.

A The measurement needs to be specific and be able to yield feedback in small, incremental steps. The data needs to be easy to collect and show the types of small changes that will encourage the student to keep trying. Growth on a yearly achievement test is too massive and not timely feedback. ***Assessments*** such as weekly growth in words-per-minute written, amount of time on task, or improvement on a self-editing checklist are more user-friendly (i.e., improves from an average of four minutes to six minutes, goes from 50% to 65%, shows better attitude by asking for help at least once a day when stuck). These types of assessments easily show movement from the baseline data to new target goal.

Case 6: Converting "Five Reasons" results to a DATA goal:

Tosha is a bright child who is failing in writing and math. She reads very well orally and seems to have no problem comprehending what she reads. She is shy and tends to pull back from the group. She is reluctant to join into playground games.

Tosha's biggest issue is not turning in work or turning things in that are incomplete. This happens about 40% of the time. She seems to be working hard but just doesn't get the jobs accomplished.

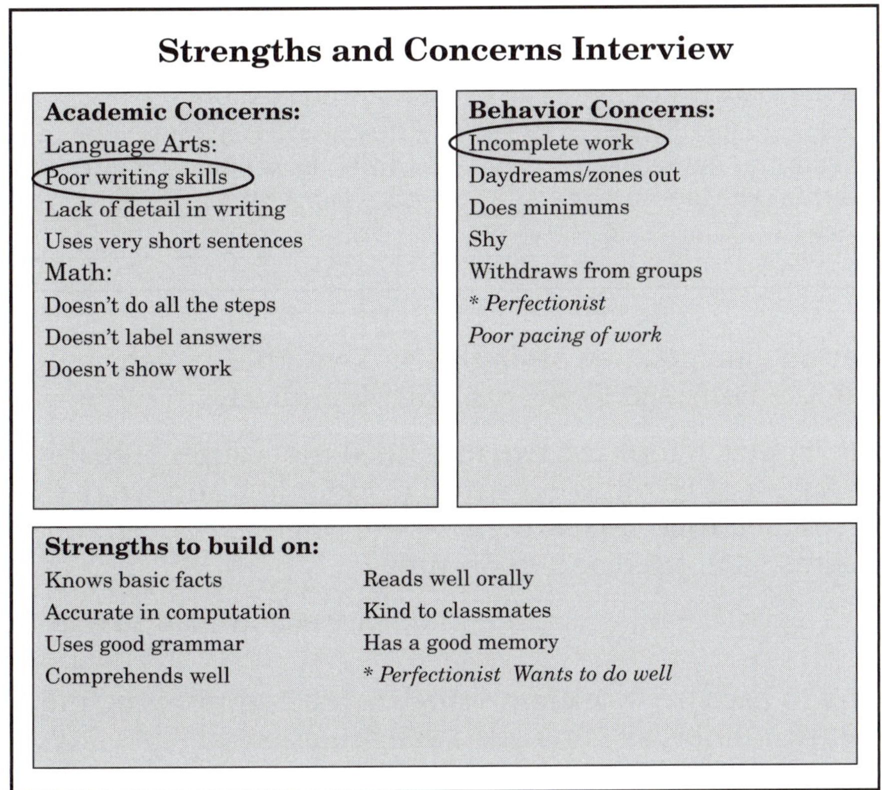

Strengths and Concerns Interview

Academic Concerns:
Language Arts:
Poor writing skills
Lack of detail in writing
Uses very short sentences
Math:
Doesn't do all the steps
Doesn't label answers
Doesn't show work

Behavior Concerns:
Incomplete work
Daydreams/zones out
Does minimums
Shy
Withdraws from groups
* *Perfectionist*
Poor pacing of work

Strengths to build on:
Knows basic facts
Accurate in computation
Uses good grammar
Comprehends well
Reads well orally
Kind to classmates
Has a good memory
* *Perfectionist Wants to do well*

* Both the *Perfectionist* and self-pacing problems were added to the list as the "Five Reasons" analysis was taking place. This is a working document not limited to use as the beginning step.

The teacher circled two areas to start with: poor writing skills as the key academic concern and lack of complete work as the behavioral concern. The coach and teacher choose to start with the writing problem as they begin the Five Reasons analysis. They will then do the same process with the work completion concern. It is not uncommon to have the two conversations lead to the same root cause. In Tosha's case, the conversation leads into the second issue of work completion as part of the "Five Reasons Deep" analysis of the writing skills.

Case 6: Tosha has poor writing and does not complete work.

Coach says:	Teacher says:
1. Why is Tosha failing writing?	1. She consistently hands in incomplete work.
2. Why doesn't she get finished?	2. She zones out during assignments.
3. What could be causing that zoning?	3. I have no idea.
4. Some kids need a mental break, others don't have enough challenge. Could these be reasons for Tosha?	4. Not really. She is bright and capable but never gives the impression she is bored. In fact, I'd say she's more of a perfectionist than anything.
5. How might this perfectionist tendency be influencing her work or lack of it?	5. Well, she wants it to be perfect and she takes too long to get it there.
6. Why do you think she's taking so long?	6. I really don't know.
7. Do you think she's vague about what "good" should look like, so she keeps redoing, or do you think she lacks the skill of pacing herself?	7. Either one of those might be true. She does want to do well but she just can't move off the dime and get the work done.

As the conversation emerges, new strengths and weaknesses can come up. Feel free to add them to the original Strengths and Concerns Interview Sheet.

In this example, the coach took the two identified root causes of inability to pace work and difficulty with a clear idea of what "good writing" looks like and wove them together for the start of the DATA goal. She then linked these to the original concern of getting only 40% of the writing assignments completed and in on time.

The original DATA goal set by the coach and teacher sounded like this . . .

D—If we teach Tosha to pace her work and visualize the end result before she begins writing
A—she will increase the number of completed assignments
T—within the next five weeks.
A—This will be measured by grades of "C" or better on daily writing assignments. At least 80% of her assignments will be complete, and there will be no late assignments.

After showing this DATA goal to Tosha's mother and to Tosha, the group adjusted the goal because Tosha said she was feeling too rushed and would rather throw the papers away than hand in something she was ashamed of.

The revised DATA goal now sounds like this:

D—If we teach Tosha to pace her work and visualize the end result before she begins writing
A—she will increase the number of completed assignments
T—within the next five weeks.
A—This will be measured by an average of "3" out of "4" on the writing assignments. At least 60% of her assignments will be completed on time. Tosha will be able to estimate how much longer she will need to complete the other 40% of the assignments and justify why she needs this additional time.

This revision accomplished several things. It clarified what success would look like for all team members and allowed the parent and student to own the goal because their concerns were heard and responded to. Never underestimate the power of "buy-in," especially by the person who has to make the biggest change.

Once the DATA goal is clear, the teacher may feel he/she knows enough strategies to get started without taking the case to an "expert team."

If no formal team meeting is required to brainstorm interventions, the coach, teacher, and family get together to complete the process of deciding how the adults will support Tosha's intervention plan. They will also identify the exact data collection techniques that will be used to determine if the strategies they agree to are being successful.

Part of the data collection also needs to compare Tosha with other students in the class. This gives the goal a frame of reference. If most kids can score "3s" on the rubric, it probably doesn't make sense to set the target higher than that for Tosha right now.

If a formal meeting is needed, the coach and teacher discuss the following roles and responsibilities for getting everyone ready for the problem-solving meeting.

Step 5. Cooperatively identify people with the most expertise to serve as members capable of coming up with ideas that specifically suit Tosha's case.

Step 6. Decide who will inform people of the time and place of the meeting. Decide who will help Tosha's parents understand their role at the meeting.

Step 7. Decide who will make the courtesy follow-up call to Tosha's family to see if they need assistance in getting their ideas ready for the meeting.

Step 8. Decide who will fill the role of student advocate before and during the meeting.

Step 9. Distribute Baseline and Planning form and work samples to all team members so they can come prepared with targeted interventions for Tosha.

Let's Practice Data Goals

DATA goals select the target behaviors for the adults and the student, as well as identify the specific evidence that will measure the student's progress.

The next few practice pages are actual DATA goals written by first-time coaches. The examples were selected because they represent typical errors people make as they begin to learn this new skill. Use the rubric below to help you analyze these DATA goals.

	Not acceptable 1	Marginal 2	Acceptable 3	Excellent 4
Do Differently	Only labels the problem	Focus is on teaching skills without a new twist, or an accommodation vs. intervention	Suggests a specific new strategy for solving the problem	Intervention idea that develops independence. Focused on student-learning
Student Achievement Target	Does not address a student change	Student change does not seem reasonable or does not reflect the original problem	Student change seems reasonable (but may emphasize compliance)	Reasonable student change identified that focuses on a life skill
Time	No time frame given	Time frame is too long or too short for the target identified	Time is probably reasonable and no longer than six weeks	Definitely a reasonable time frame
Assessment	No assessment data collection identified	Data collection is vague or cannot reveal a pattern in a six week period or less	Teacher collects assessment data that measures growth in small increments	Teacher and student assess growth together in small data increments

Example 1: Jerome's transitions

Jerome is an extremely bright third-grade student with a few autistic-like tendencies that make starting and stopping activities difficult for him. The baseline data shows that Jerome has various degrees of meltdowns on an average of six times a day. Getting off the bus, coming to reading circle, going to lunch, coming in from recess, going to any fine arts class, going to the media center, and getting ready to go home are the high risk times. To a lesser degree, he has difficulty changing activities within the classroom. He often seems unable to stop what he is currently involved in when the class is moving on to something else (about 50% of the time).

Original DATA goal:

If we allow Jerome to leave class two minutes early, he will be able to make room-to-room transitions within four weeks. 80% of the time he will change classes without being a disruption to himself or others. This will be assessed by teacher feedback.

How would you improve this goal?

Analyzing what you just read:

	Not acceptable 1	Marginal 2	Acceptable 3	Excellent 4
Do Differently	Only labels the problem	Focus is on teaching skills without a new twist, or an accommodation vs. intervention	Suggests a specific new strategy for solving the problem	Intervention idea that develops independence. Focused on student-learning
Student Achievement Target	Does not address a student change	Student change does not seem reasonable or does not reflect the original problem	Student change seems reasonable (but may emphasize compliance)	Reasonable student change identified that focuses on a life skill
Time	No time frame given	Time frame is too long or too short for the target identified	Time is probably reasonable and no longer than six weeks	Definitely a reasonable time frame
Assessment	No assessment data collection identified	Data collection is vague or cannot reveal a pattern in a six week period or less	Teacher collects assessment data that measures growth in small increments	Teacher and student assess growth together in small data increments

Do Differently–2 (marginal):

Reminding Jerome to leave class two minutes early is not an intervention. It is an accommodation and probably a good one, but it does not go far enough to develop new skills or skills for independence in Jerome. The teachers are doing the work, not Jerome.

Student Achievement–3 (acceptable):

"Jerome will make room-to-room transitions" is a clear and specific student change. It only deals with part of the problematic behavior, but it is a reasonable place to start. The in-room transitions are less difficult and could be a more successful starting place.

Time–3 (acceptable):

"Within four weeks" is clear, specific and *probably* reasonable, considering that the parent and Jerome thought he had the ability to understand and comply. There was hesitation on the teacher's part that four weeks would be enough time. (I would always opt for a goal that is likely to be achieved so the student sees himself as a success early in the game.)

Assessment–2 (marginal):

Teacher feedback is a vague and subjective criterion, unless it is in relation to some kind of a rubric or checklist. How is a teacher, Jerome or his parents supposed to get the same clear idea of what "acceptable transitions" look like if it is not spelled out? Acceptable and non-disruptive to one person may not be the same for another.

One Possibility for a Revised DATA goal:

D—If we teach Jerome to develop and critique his own plan for making transitions from one activity to another
A—he will increase his ability to get stopped and started on a new activity
T—within the next six weeks.
A—He will decrease his meltdown behavior during transitions by 10% (screaming, kicking and/or shouting) and will be able to start activities within 45 seconds of most children in the class, as assessed by feedback using a teacher and student-developed checklist and daily scorecard kept by both.

Example 2: Diego

Diego is a bright seventeen-year-old gifted athlete who shines on the court or field but morphs into an entirely different person in the classroom. All the confidence and drive that flows from him in physical events disappears when it comes to academics. Diego doesn't seem to get the fact that there is a relationship between the amount of effort he puts into his work and the grades he gets. He misses lots of school and thinks the teachers have it in for him.

DATA goal:

If we get Diego to come to school regularly and hand in his work his grades will improve.

What would you do to improve this DATA goal?

Analyzing what you just read:

	Not acceptable 1	Marginal 2	Acceptable 3	Excellent 4
Do Differently	Only labels the problem	Focus is on teaching skills without a new twist, or an accommodation vs. intervention	Suggests a specific new strategy for solving the problem	Intervention idea that develops independence. Focused on student-learning
Student Achievement Target	Does not address a student change	Student change does not seem reasonable or does not reflect the original problem	Student change seems reasonable (but may emphasize compliance)	Reasonable student change identified that focuses on a life skill
Time	No time frame given	Time frame is too long or too short for the target identified	Time is probably reasonable and no longer than six weeks	Definitely a reasonable time frame
Assessment	No assessment data collection identified	Data collection is vague or cannot reveal a pattern in a six week period or less	Teacher collects assessment data that measures growth in small increments	Teacher and student assess growth together in small data increments

Do Differently–1 (not acceptable):

Coming to school is never an intervention or treatment because absenteeism is a symptom, not a cause of the problems. The DATA goal has to address the fact that he doesn't see the relationship between his effort and his results.

Student Achievement–3 (acceptable):

Raising Diego's grades is a reasonable and desirable goal (but it won't happen with this DATA goal if the intervention doesn't change from just getting him to school more often).

Time–1 (not acceptable):

There is no timeframe given in this DATA goal.

Assessment–1 (not acceptable):

There is no data or evidence being collected to verify whether his grades are improving or not.

Possibility for a Revised DATA goal:

D—If we teach Diego to track his own progress so he can see the cause/effect relationship between how he studies and completes work and the grades that result,
A—we believe Diego's grades will improve
T—within a six week period
A—by 20% as measured by grades on test results. Diego and his teacher will track how long and the type of studying Diego did on one chart, and his grades on each quiz on another chart. Weekly conferences will help Diego analyze how the two charts correlate.

Example 3: Trenton

Trenton is a very capable seventh grader who has outstanding social skills. He is loved by one and all, but this strength is also his teacher's concern. Trenton cannot seem to figure out when to stop socializing and start working. His last on-task audit revealed that he spends almost half of his time messing around. Surprisingly enough, all of his assignments are complete, but the quality of his written work is very poor. The only thing that saves his grades is perfect scores on tests. One of the main concerns of his teachers is the learning of the students who sit around Trenton.

DATA goal:

If we provide incentives for Trenton to produce high quality work, he will stop distracting others (decrease from 52% of the time to 20% of the time) within four weeks as assessed by work samples.

Analyzing what you just read:

	Not acceptable 1	Marginal 2	Acceptable 3	Excellent 4
Do Differently	Only labels the problem	Focus is on teaching skills without a new twist, or an accommodation vs. intervention	Suggests a specific new strategy for solving the problem	Intervention idea that develops independence. Focused on student-learning
Student Achievement Target	Does not address a student change	Student change does not seem reasonable or does not reflect the original problem	Student change seems reasonable (but may emphasize compliance)	Reasonable student change identified that focuses on a life skill
Time	No time frame given	Time frame is too long or too short for the target identified	Time is probably reasonable and no longer than six weeks	Definitely a reasonable time frame
Assessment	No assessment data collection identified	Data collection is vague or cannot reveal a pattern in a six week period or less	Teacher collects assessment data that measures growth in small increments	Teacher and student assess growth together in small data increments

Do Differently–2 (marginal):

"... provide incentives ..." teaches Trenton no new skill. In fact, it could teach him some things about being manipulated and manipulative if this plan is not handled well. Rewards and punishments have their place in a plan, but they cannot "be the plan." Trenton needs to be taught some new skills and strategies.

Student Achievement–3 (acceptable):

The target for improvement is "he will stop distracting others." This change is reasonable. It may be more helpful to the class than to Trenton, however. This goal emphasizes compliance. There's nothing wrong with compliance but it has to go *further than that* to be a strong DATA goal.

Time–4 (excellent):

His parent and teachers thought "within four weeks" seemed to be a reasonable and likely time frame considering the goal.

Assessment–2 (marginal):

" . . . decrease in disruptions, from 52% of the time to 20% of the time as assessed by work samples." This assessment's greatest weakness is a mismatch between what is being measured and the data that is being collected. How can you measure disruptions by using work samples?

Possibility for a Revised DATA goal:

D—If we help Trenton put a plan together for both improving his work quality and decreasing class disruptions,
A—we will see his written work improve and disruptions in class decrease
T—within four weeks.
A—Grades on written work will increase one level on the writing rubric. We will also see a decrease in disruptive behavior (from 52% of the time to 20%) as measured by a time-on-task chart kept by both the teacher and Trenton.

Example 4: Jessie

Jessie is a 14-year-old freshman with average intelligence. She is well-liked by peers and has a happy-go-lucky attitude about everything except school. She has a particularly difficult time with math and is presently getting an "F" in it. Jessie gets very confused about what process to use when doing real-life math problem-solving. She learns better visually and is willing to use manipulatives to figure out math problems. Jessie is a good reader, although she says she does not enjoy reading. When she has to listen, especially in large groups, Jessie tends to get confused and lose focus.

DATA goal:

I will work with Jesse to find alternative assignments. By the end of the semester, Jessie will have completed work that is more complex and will show more enthusiasm for school.

How would you improve this DATA goal?

Analyzing what you just read:

	Not acceptable 1	Marginal 2	Acceptable 3	Excellent 4
Do Differently	Only labels the problem	Focus is on teaching skills without a new twist, or an accommodation vs. intervention	Suggests a specific new strategy for solving the problem	Intervention idea that develops independence. Focused on student-learning
Student Achievement Target	Does not address a student change	Student change does not seem reasonable or does not reflect the original problem	Student change seems reasonable (but may emphasize compliance)	Reasonable student change identified that focuses on a life skill
Time	No time frame given	Time frame is too long or too short for the target identified	Time is probably reasonable and no longer than six weeks	Definitely a reasonable time frame
Assessment	No assessment data collection identified	Data collection is vague or cannot reveal a pattern in a six week period or less	Teacher collects assessment data that measures growth in small increments	Teacher and student assess growth together in small data increments

Do Differently–2 (marginal):

"I will work with Jessie to find alternative assignments" is an accommodation, not an intervention. It focuses on unclear adult activity rather than an effort to put specific new skills of independence in place.

Student Achievement–2 (marginal):

"Jessie will have completed work that is more complex and will show more enthusiasm for school" is too vague. Completing work was not a problem for Jessie. Understanding what she is working on *is* a problem even at the present level of complexity. Work completion is seldom a good target in and of itself. Demonstrating some type of understanding as a result of doing work is what we need to see.

Time–2 (marginal):

"By the end of the semester" is probably too long, unless the end of the semester is less than six weeks away (which it was not in this case).

Assessment–1 (not acceptable):

How her work or her enthusiasm is to be assessed and judged is not mentioned in this goal.

Possibility for a Revised DATA goal:

D—If we teach Jessie to use graphic organizers to help her visualize and analyze math problems,
A—her math scores will improve
T—within six weeks.
A—Evidence of improvement will be moving from "F" to an average of "C" on her daily work and quizzes. Jessie will also be able to identify where she is making her mistakes at least 50% of the time.

Chapter Three

An Ounce of Prevention or First Step of Cure

Intervention Pyramid

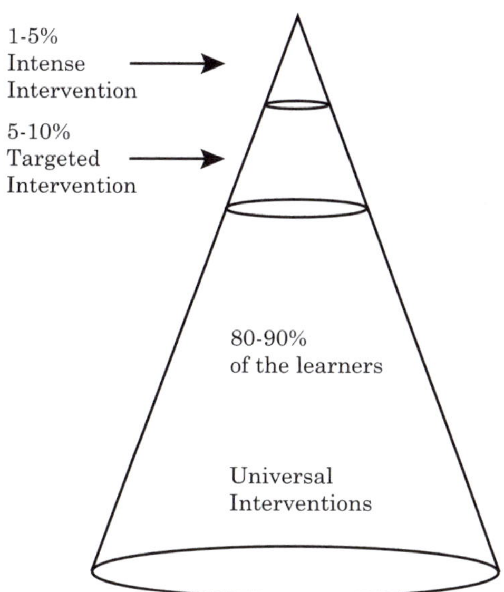

How do we reach *all* students: the ones who struggle with reading and writing, the ones who are bored or more interested in social life than school work, the ones who are unmotivated and refuse to do their assignments?

Coaches and the problem-solving experts must work hand-in-hand in order to operate efficiently. The coaches rely upon the "experts" on the faculty to feed them the latest research about root causes for problems. The problem-solving experts depend upon the coaches and referring teachers to provide them with a quality analysis of problems and clear, specific DATA goals to help guide intervention selections.

Once a coach and referring teacher turn over the baseline data and DATA goal to the problem-solving expert, the job changes from analyzing the problem to designing a list of appropriate interventions based upon the data received.

Designing a quality intervention plan requires a thinking process that ensures that "experts" have considered a continuum of interventions. The task is to determine the least intensive interventions and accommodations that have the greatest likelihood of making a difference. Consistently using strategies that have a high probability of success for all types of learners is the first step in reducing school failures. This problem-solving logic is the thinking behind the "Three-tier Model of School Supports" (Adelman & Taylor, 1998; Sugai, Horner, & Gresham, 2002).

If every teacher in a school system would put universal research-based strategies in place, the number of students who appear to be "at risk" would drop dramatically. When a student is referred, one of the first things to check is whether these fundamental strategies are consistently being used with this student. Intervention plans built on these universal designs will not only help the student in question but also benefit other students in the class at the same time.

This chapter will describe ideas for six areas that have been shown to be effective with 80–90% of the learners:

Creating a safe and welcoming environment

Focusing the learners' attention

Pacing lessons

Chunking material

Planning practice and rehearsal

Providing feedback and reinforcement

These areas easily lend themselves to implementation regardless of grade, subject, or type of learner served. Later in Chapter Four, we will look at interventions specifically geared to learners who need intensive small-group or individual plans added to the basic intervention plans.

1. Create an Inviting and Safe Learning Environment

The brain is programmed to turn part of itself off when challenge turns into threat.

When the brain is challenged and actively involved in a non-threatening situation, it can handle very complex tasks and problem-solving. The brain is programmed to turn part of itself off when challenge turns into threat. This is called downshifting (Caine & Caine, 1991).

Dominic and Eric were sitting in my office when I came back from my meeting. It was the fourth time in two weeks that they had been thrown out of second period.

"Okay, guys, what are you in for today?"

Dominic slides down in his seat and mutters, "Nuthin'."

"Is it the same nuthin' as on Tuesday?"

Eric erupts, "Mrs. Searle, there's just no pleasin' that woman. She called on me and I gave her my best answer. You know what she says to me? 'You're just not concentrating!' The heck I'm not concentrating. I just don't get it, that's what. She's a lousy teacher!"

"That's a fact," pipes in Dominic. "She makes everybody feel stupid unless you're a brainiac pet. I just stopped trying in there."

The sad part of this situation was that I knew these boys were speaking the truth. This teacher had enough knowledge of her content to be considered outstanding, but she was not even an average teacher for young learners.

Master teachers are the people who can inspire you to go beyond what you thought were your limits.

Master teachers are people who can get you to go where you didn't think you could. They inspire you to stretch yourself. They can make you believe you can succeed. Creating a classroom environment where each brain perceives a challenge is the mark of a great teacher. The big question is, "How do I make my class challenging to all when any given assignment is perceived as boring by a few and threatening by others, even though it challenges most?"

What do great teachers do to create a challenge and reduce threat? We have to consider three areas: academic, social, and emotional.

Eric and Dominic were being threatened in all three areas. Academically they were having difficulty understanding the work. Socially they were being embarrassed in front of their friends. Emotionally they were in trouble, because they were being told that if they would try harder, they would get it. They had been trying and still didn't get it—and concluded: "I'm not smart enough to get it. No sense trying."

Ideas for creating a safe and welcoming environment:

The way you choose to treat the students will have everything to do with the way they respond to you and to others in the class.

A predictable, consistent environment makes students feel safe and cared for.

1. Make **students feel welcome** in your room by greeting them at the door with some personal recognition. "Hi, Gary. How's that new puppy?" It doesn't have to be much of a statement to let the student know you are interested in them.
2. Maintain a **structured, predictable learning environment** (schedules, basic rules, consistent procedures, breaks). This helps students feel safe because the environment is predictable and consistent. Set up a class for success by following these guidelines:
    a. Be clear about what you want students to learn, why the skills you teach are important to their lives beyond school, and how you plan to give them feedback about their learning.
    b. Establish clear routines and procedures for classroom management. Teach and practice these skills regularly, just like you do for the rest of your curriculum.
    c. Praise and correct immediately after the action, and be specific about what is right and what needs to be corrected.
    d. Give students opportunities to correct errors so they learn from these errors rather than brush them off or feel inferior because of having made a mistake.
    e. Help students see how their good efforts help create a productive class and tell them how much you appreciate it. Let them know you support them.
3. Telling kids to "try harder" is not an intervention. **Modeling the correct response,** having them model it back, and then practicing the new behavior or skill until it is comfortably in place helps create an emotionally safe learning environment.
4. **Re-teaching should be done using a different style** than the first way it was presented (i.e., use a visual instead of

just verbal, make the example more concrete, break it down into smaller steps). This reduces the risk of having students blame themselves and then just giving up.

Feeling physically, emotionally and socially safe and welcome is essential to efficient learning.

5. When asking for public responses, protect the students' dignity by giving them a chance to quickly discuss their answers with the person sitting next to them. Teachers have everything to gain by providing these **brief oral rehearsals** because calling on one student only engages that child. Having the students verbalize their answers before calling on one person engages the entire class and gives reluctant learners a tiny rehearsal to check their thinking before committing to an answer. Building confidence is as important as building the skills.

Assume the best about students' intentions, even if their actions would have you believe they do not care or do not want to learn.

6. **Assume the best about the student's intentions** even if their actions would have you believe they do not care or do not want to learn. What you believe about a student will determine how effective you can be with him. If you believe him to be stupid and hostile, the way you approach him will most likely bring out these characteristics. If you believe the student wants to learn but is just having a hard time understanding what you want from him, your approach and the student's response are likely to be much more positive in the long run (Smith, Rick, 2004).
7. Take care of yourself. Cranky and dead-tired teachers can't expect to perform at the top of their game. Take time to do something fun and relaxing each day. Work as a member of a team at school so you don't have to reinvent the wheel for every lesson and problem. Healthy, rested teachers have a better chance of keeping their **senses of humor and positive attitudes** intact—basic requirements for a good learning environment.

You have to model respect yourself, if you intend to see it from the students.

When I was about to lose my temper, I often used this **mental model** for myself. I envisioned the student's parents or the superintendent standing right behind him saying, "He is counting on you to do and say the right thing for him." I then addressed the issue firmly but didn't say anything I would be reluctant to say with those adults present in the room. The more I controlled my stress level, the more effective I was able to be with the students. Insist on an atmosphere of respect for both adults and other students (courtesy, listening to each other, expressing opinions respectfully, and honoring the opinions of others). Respectfully stop any violation of this every time you see it. If someone is allowed to make fun of a classmate even once in a while, you have no rule about respect. Remember, you have to model it yourself, if you intend to see it from the students.

Kids and parents need to know you are on their side.

8. Keep in **contact with the students' parents/guardians** (i.e., phone calls when things are going right, home visits, regular newsletters or e-mails). These things will pay off by helping the students see that you care about them. When you have to make the call about things that are problems they will already know you are on their side.

2. Focusing Attention

Once the teacher makes the students feel safe and accepted, they will be more likely to pay attention. This attention can be greatly enhanced when the brain is primed to focus in on a specific topic. Madeline Hunter referred to this as "establishing set." Establishing set is simply giving the students a specific focus to pay attention to and learn by the end of the lesson and giving them the reason to want to do it. Focusing attention on essential elements reduces the complexity of the task (Vargas, et. al., 2002; Walberg, 1999).

Focusing attention on essential elements reduces the complexity of the task. (Vargas, et. al., 2002; Walberg, 1999).

Getting focused is critical to learning. Let's say you are looking for your glasses (a frequent ritual at my house). As you go through your house, your brain takes in hundreds of images, but it has been primed to ignore irrelevant items and focus on what it perceives to be most important at that moment (LaBarge, 1995). When a teacher helps students focus on what is important, the ability to ignore distracting information is enhanced.

Ideas for focusing students:

When a teacher helps students focus on what is important, the ability to ignore distracting information is more likely to occur.

1. Post the **purpose of the lesson** on the board and discuss it at the beginning of the class (i.e., "At the end of the period I am going to ask you to answer this question: *Who really won the Civil War?*" or "I want you to tell me three ways of sorting these ideas by the end of the class."). Students should be able to restate what they are learning in their own terms.

2. Give students an **overview** of the class before it starts, emphasizing what difference knowing this material could make to their lives. If the topic matters to students, they will be much more creative and on-task than students who don't care or are just working for grades.
3. Give students "**advance organizers**" which are visual displays or charts of the key concepts to be learned. These tools focus students on what is important (Darch & Carnine, 1986).

Have the students fill in parts of the organizer or study guide during the class to keep their attention on these key issues.

4. Asking a question about the key topic before instruction focuses the students on what they already know about the topic (**prior knowledge**). Then ask what questions they would like to have answered about this concept. This can be done using a graphic organizer like a KWL chart (what I **K**now, what I **W**ant to know, what I **L**earned from the lesson.) Make a transparency of what the class members think they know about the topic and then add or eliminate items as they learn more and discard misconceptions (Walberg, 1999).
5. Post and refer to an "**Essential Understanding**" that focuses students on the patterns and generalizations that will link several skills and concepts together for them (McTighe & Wiggins, 1999).
6. Give a **pre-assessment** and let the students change and refine their answers as the lesson progresses. Never give a grade for a pre-assessment. It is designed to help the students focus on what they need to know and learn during the lesson (Walberg, 1999).
7. Tell students they will be expected to **summarize** the lesson several times throughout the lesson or give you an exit card at the end of the class (ten-word summary on the front and a question they still have about the topic on the back).

3. Pacing of the Lesson

The first year I taught eighth-grade English, I had a group of students in fourth period made up of struggling readers and writers. It seemed I worked twice as hard during that period and made half the progress. The kids were cooperative enough after we figured out that we liked each other (most of the time), but the learning curve was steep for them and I could see I was not helping their frustration levels.

One day Vincent threw his pencil down and said, "I've had it with this class."

"I can see that. What's the problem?" I replied as I tried to keep the rest of the class from joining in on what I saw as a budding rebellion.

"I can't do this stuff. Just when I think I have it, you jump in there and throw one more thing at me. I'm drowning here. Can't you slow down?"

I had fallen into the trap of feeling the pressure to cover the material. I was making the mistake of moving too fast over too much. Most of us, when asked if we think this improves student learning, will admit that we know cramming is counter-productive but for some reason we keep doing it.

Research shows that the brain does poorly at continuous high levels of attention. We need time to process the information we are learning. Sometimes teachers think we can make learning happen faster by telling the students what connections and patterns they should see. This is an unproductive strategy, because meaning is always generated internally, not externally. After each new learning experience, we need to give students time for the learning to "imprint" in their memory (Jensen, 1998).

Research shows that the brain does poorly at continuous high levels of attention. We need time to process the information we are learning.

Ideas for pacing the lesson:

Lecture or direct teach no more minutes than the students are old.

1. Keep the passive-receptive parts of the lesson coming in short bursts with processing times in between. One rule of thumb is, "Lecture or direct teach no more minutes than the students are old." This keeps the **pace lively and age-appropriate.** This rule only applies up to 20–25 minutes. After that generally you reach the point of no return even with adults. The interest in the material and the level of active participation does influence this guideline. If you are really "on" and your class is engaged, you may stretch this time by a few minutes. If you or your topic are as boring as watching golf on TV (my opinion only), think about cutting it to half the number of minutes.
2. After new material is introduced, plan **small group or paired discussions** to allow students to process and organize the information before adding new ideas that could interfere with the original learning.
3. Plan for **reflection time** to link new information to what is already known. This can be done by writing in journals, using graphic organizers, or verbally sharing insights with others.
4. **Gauge the pacing of the lesson to the newness and difficulty of the material.** Material that is new and/or difficult requires processing time of two to five minutes every ten to fifteen minutes. Review of old-hat material may require only a minute or so every twenty minutes (Jensen 1998).
5. The more boring and irrelevant the material, the more **fast-paced and interactive** the lesson must be in order to keep learner attention focused.
6. **Adding color, movement, and verbal cues** to a lesson can increase attention to important elements as you teach (Zentall & Kruczek, 1988).

4. Chunking Material to See Patterns

Research shows that seven-year-olds can typically hold three chunks of information in working memory and eleven-year-olds can hold five. The ability to accurately recall chunks of information generally increases by one for every two years of age (Pascual-Leone, 1970).

If what is to be learned appears to the learner to be isolated units of information, working memory overload can happen early in a lesson.

Chunks are defined as bits of information like single letters, digits, or any meaningful unit of information. If what is to be learned appears to the learner to be isolated units of information (unrelated names, dates and places, vocabulary out of context, etc.) working memory overload can happen early in a lesson. If the teacher helps students make their own connections and see patterns, the amount of information contained in each chunk increases. The teacher can successfully present more material in a lesson if the students are given reflection time and opportunities to make connections and see patterns (Wolfe, 2001).

Ideas for chunking information:

1. Teach students to use **graphic organizers** such as webs, charts, maps, diagrams, picture/word note taking, to depict relationships and show patterns.
2. **Highlight** key concepts in one color and related details in another color to make patterns of main idea/detail more obvious.
3. Use **role-playing and skits** to organize information and see relationships to real-world issues.
4. Have the students tell **personal stories** of how they might use this information in their own lives or how this information reminds them of something they have done in the past.
5. Use **comparison and contrast** to see how the new information is like something they know. More sophisticated versions of the compare/contrast skill are creating categories, metaphors, similes, analogies.
6. Use **mnemonics** to link one idea to another (HOMES helps you remember the names of the Great Lakes, FACE names the spaces on a music staff, etc.). This technique is useful for remembering facts that are useful but do not require deep thinking (i.e., order of operations in math, names of the planets, etc.).
7. Give oral previews to the lesson to focus on the upcoming **patterns.** Have the students fill in study guides as pieces of the pattern emerge in the lesson. Have them summarize the pattern at the end.

5. Practice

Memory is not formed at the moment information is taken in. Unless the memory is linked to a powerful emotion, forming a memory is more of a dynamic process that requires rehearsals over a period of time. By recalling our experiences and linking them to our prior knowledge, we increase our ability to retain information.

Mastery of any skill or content requires practice, but there's good practice and there's bad practice. One saying goes, "Practice makes perfect but only if the practice is perfect." Other people say, "Practice makes permanent." Given this adage, if you practice the wrong things in the wrong ways, all you've done is dig yourself a hole. Unlearning bad thinking patterns and replacing them with better ones is a more painful process than learning it correctly to begin with. Using rote and elaborative rehearsals correctly can keep you from having that problem.

Rote rehearsal is intensive repetition of information or action in order to get the learning to the automatic level.

Rote rehearsal is intensive repetition of information or action in order to get learning to the automatic level. Driving a car, decoding words, and knowing basic math facts are examples of skills and procedures that need to be practiced to automatic levels. These automatic levels free up brainpower and make it easier to pay attention to deeper kinds of thinking processes.

Elaborative rehearsal is meant to develop deeper understandings by expanding on a concept. This type of rehearsal makes personal connections and focuses on relationships and patterns in order to improve the brain's ability to store and retrieve information.

Elaborative rehearsal is meant to develop the deeper understandings by expanding on a concept.

Ideas for practice and rehearsal

Introducing a second new skill too soon can interrupt the learning and the strength of the memory of the first skill.

1. Use **modeling and guided practice** of a few skills at a time to solidify understanding before asking students to go for speed and accuracy. Introducing a second new skill too soon can interrupt the learning and the strength of the memory of the first skill (Squire & Kandel, 2000).
2. When going for speed and accuracy, the first **practice sessions** should be close together and frequent. Over time, practice sessions should be shortened and spaced farther apart (Healy, J.M., 1990).
3. Have students verbalize what they read and hear (Silven and Vauras, 1992). Students who **think aloud** about what is happening in their head as they learn are better able to understand and summarize the information they need to remember.
4. The brain loves **uniqueness and variety.** Changing the type of practice not only grabs students' attention but also can create multiple pathways in the brain for storage and retrieval.

When rehearsals on the same concept are varied and show relationships, the learning deepens because the concept is expanded, not just practiced. Research shows that elaborative rehearsal enables students not only to understand the concepts better but allows them to recall it more easily (Pressley, Symons, McDaniel, Snyder & Turner, 1988).

Here is an example of **elaborative rehearsal:**

a. Vocabulary is introduced by having the students tell what they already know or think they know about the word—connect to prior knowledge.
b. The second rehearsal asks students to give two examples of the vocabulary word (i.e., heroic—examples would be firefighters, people who stand up for their friends, Mother Teresa, etc.).
c. On the third day the students create two sets of flashcards. The first set has the word on one side and the dictionary definition on the other. The second set of flashcards has a paraphrased definition on just one side of the card. Homework is to match the paraphrased definition to the vocabulary word.
d. On the fourth day students draw a symbol or picture on the back of the paraphrased definition card. Kids can now use the two sets of cards to study their vocabulary by matching these cards in a number of ways.
e. The next rehearsal asks the students to use each word in a sentence and use a colored highlighter to emphasize the vocabulary word. One partner reads his sentence and the other partner gives the definition.
f. Students separate the flashcards into three categories. Name the categories and explain why each word belongs there.
g. Sort the words on a Venn diagram to show ways they are alike and different.

Basically, elaborative rehearsal challenges the brain to make a variety of new connections. Not every vocabulary word studied would deserve this kind of depth, but some would. This kind of thinking is also used to develop concepts and skills. The same process can be used with a variety of note taking strategies.

Elaborative rehearsal takes learning to a new level of sophistication by asking students to do things like visualize, classify, find examples, analyze for errors, use symbols to represent the subject, make up a song or rap about it, and apply it to a real-world situation. Each rehearsal variation creates a deeper, more complete memory of how this information fits into the scheme of important things.

6. Feedback and Reinforcement

"The most powerful single modification that enhances student achievement is feedback. The simplest prescription for improving education must be dollops of feedback," says researcher John Hattie (1992). The focus has to be on student learning.

Many times I hear teachers ask, "Well, what if the kids just don't care?" Just allowing yourself to think that thought creates a handicap for a teacher. If you do not believe the student wants to learn, you have already partially resigned yourself to feeling helpless and your actions toward that student will show it. You have to believe in your students in order to be effective with them. This "assume the best" attitude on your part will not stop the students from trying to convince you that they really don't care, but it will stop you from acting like you are not on their side.

One way to help students see that you are on their side is to develop feedback that clearly sends that supportive and positive message. Feedback that says, "I believe you can and will do well on this if I just show you how" has a more positive effect on learning than feedback that says, "I will judge your work and give you a grade on it."

Research shows that adolescents define caring teachers as those who communicate directly and regularly with them about their academic progress and make sure they understand what has been taught (Wentzel, 2002).

Ideas for feedback and reinforcement:

1. Demonstrate the exact steps or skills that need to be in place. This way there is no question about the **exact expectations for behavior or for academic excellence.** Checklists and rubrics are great helps and sample papers and demonstrations are essential to help clarify the meaning of those documents.
2. **Be *specific*** about what the student is doing right and wrong.

   "When you are looking out of the window, it doesn't count as being on task. I want you to look at your paper."

   "Your topic sentence tells exactly what the rest of the paragraph is about. Great. Now let's look at the kinds of adjectives you have. Three of your four sentences have several adjectives, and two of the sentences have very powerful ones. See if you can find the sentences that need to be upgraded, and tell me how you are planning to do that."
3. **Peer feedback** can be more motivating and useful than teacher feedback in getting lasting results (Druckman & Sweets, 1988).
4. Reprimands must be **calm, firm, consistent, and immediate** (before two minutes has passed) to be effective. Emotional or delayed reprimands may stop inappropriate behaviors but will likely make them worse in the long run (Van Houten et al., 1982).

5. **Token economies** involve giving tokens for appropriate behavior, and removing tokens for inappropriate behavior. This strategy is often effective but should not be seen as a long-term intervention. The student needs to have this technique phased out and replaced by a self-management system as soon as possible (Stokes & Osnes, 1989).
6. **Self-monitoring** the results of practice acts as motivation to continue to improve. Students charting and analyzing their own progress not only build skill and competence, but also are more likely to see themselves as successful people. Self-monitoring is much more powerful than simply using rewards or grades handed out by the teacher (Zentall, 1989; Digangi, Magg, & Rutherford, 1991). Students whose teachers overemphasize external rewards often work for the reward rather than the learning. These students are also more prone to blame an external source when things do not go well.
7. Monitoring systems need to **gather information frequently and be sensitive to small increments of growth** in order to be motivating (How long would you continue to bowl if no one was keeping score? Most people would tire much more quickly without this frequent and specific feedback to challenge them, unless they just loved the game action itself).

Chapter Four
Continuum of Research-Based Interventions

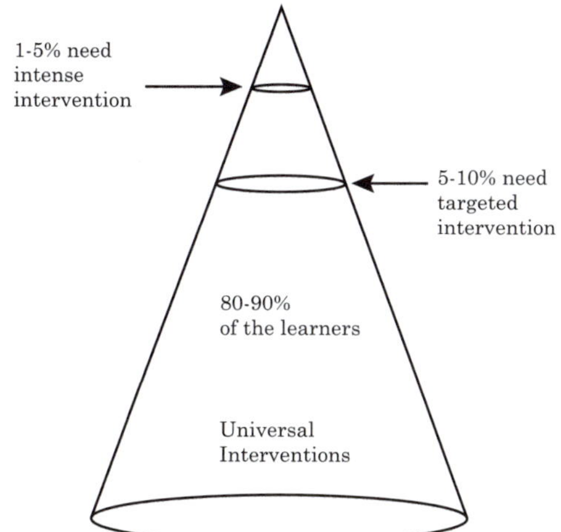

In this chapter we will use case studies to see what happens to the analysis work once the coach and the teacher turn it over to the problem-solving team. We will look at the variety of ways "problem-solving experts" can figure out which interventions to suggest, once they have the baseline data and goal for a given student.

Chapter Three focused on the kind of universal strategies that can be used as the first line of support for students. These interventions are easily implemented in general education classrooms and are beneficial for all types of learners.

To design a quality intervention plan, the problem-solving experts go through a thinking process that ensures they have considered everything from universal interventions at the bottom of the pyramid to the targeted and intensive assistance at the top. Each expert's job is to develop and expand a database of interventions and accommodations for their area of expertise as they study the newest research and best teaching practices. This database is very helpful in determining the least intensive strategies that have the greatest likelihood of making a difference for each student being referred. "Least intensive" strategies are those that can be used in a general education classroom to help a wide variety of learners. "Most intensive" strategies tend to be a different type of instruction than is found in general education classrooms, and will most likely require pull-out instruction delivered by a specialist.

If the student does not respond positively to the original level of intervention, the team slowly increases the intensity until a level is found that does work. Once the team finds a level that is successful, the goal is to fade interventions and accommodations to less intensive levels. The team works back down the pyramid to the greatest degree possible.

Problem-solving experts also design ways to track the student's progress so the team can decide if the plan is making a difference. The team's responsibility is to use this data to modify the intervention plan as needed. That adjustment may be as simple as changing the types of interventions, reconsidering the root cause, or altering the continuum of intensity up or down.

When developing an intervention plan, a spectrum of interventions must be considered. The data from the referral interview gives the problem-solving expert an idea of where on the continuum of interventions the student will need to begin. The place to start is always at the lowest reasonable level.

Questions good problem-solving experts ask themselves are:

What are the **most intensive** services a student might require?
What is the **least invasive level** that makes sense for this case?

A good analogy for this process is a medical one. When I went to an allergist, he asked me to describe my symptoms ("Five Reasons" conversation). Then, based upon this knowledge and his training, he made a hypothesis about what was causing my problem (DATA goal). Based upon this hypothesis, he prescribed the mildest form of medication that had a possibility of working. He did not jump into invasive testing or decide that I needed to be placed in the hospital for intensive breathing treatments, even though my condition might eventually land me in exactly that place. The medical-model thinking is to try incrementally stronger interventions only as the gentler treatments are found to be ineffective.

The bad part of this type of thinking is that it can take a longer time to get to the intervention that finally works. The good part of this thinking strategy is that it carefully diagnoses the problem and prevents over-reactions that, in and of themselves, could have lasting negative side effects.

With my allergist scenario, I did end up having several visits. Some of these follow-up visits included some uncomfortable tests to provide the doctor with clearer information upon which to hone the original diagnosis and make changes to my treatment. Fortunately for me, an intensive treatment plan in a clinic or a stay in a hospital was not necessary. I'm glad the doctor didn't jump right to high intensity.

Start with mild classroom interventions that become incrementally stronger until one finally works.

This is precisely what any continuum of interventions is designed to do. The idea is not to jump into a testing process with the intent of qualifying a student for an intensive special education program. The new way of thinking is to size the student up and quickly start with mild interventions that become incrementally stronger until one finally works. Along the way the team may find that specific testing results would help clarify or verify suspected problems, but the tests are not given to label the problem as much as to figure out what the next intervention should be.

My allergist identified an effective treatment, and we found that as the seasons changed I was able to decrease and actually discontinue this treatment. I seemed to be cured, only to know that as the seasons changed again I would most likely have a relapse and need to go back into treatment at some level each year.

The intent is never to deny or delay service, but to deliver targeted support that results in more success and independence for students.

This happens with school interventions as well. The goal is to fade out the interventions as success builds skills of independence. Just as the seasons of my life bring on more difficult challenges for my body, a student's increasing school demands and changing environmental factors could cause a regression that requires a "booster intervention". The intent is never to deny or delay service, but to deliver the exact types and amounts of targeted support that result in success and independence for students. We need to be watchful and prepared to deliver and withdraw support as needed.

In the case studies that follow, we will attempt to demonstrate the type of thinking that can lead to a more efficient and effective way of serving students who are struggling in school. In all but one of the cases in this chapter, the students share a common problem. Their teachers are complaining that much of the student's work is incomplete or missing. In several cases, the students are also giving the adults a lot of attitude. Even though the symptoms in these cases are similar, each student has a very different reason for displaying these behaviors. Until the correct root cause can be uncovered it is very difficult to know what to do about these problems. There is a direct correlation between identifying the root cause, writing the DATA goal in a clear and specific way, and the efficiency and effectiveness of the intervention plan.

This careful diagnostic and prescriptive process is tougher on the staff than the old "label and dispatch" model but is much more rewarding as the faculty and home work together to develop each child's potential. It is the right thing to do.

After the teacher and coach have completed the referral conference, they verify their conclusions with the parents and with the student. Once consensus is reached on the root causes of the focus issues, the team experts are given the information from the **Strengths and Concerns sheet, the Baseline Data and Planning Form and any attached work samples.** This information will guide and focus everyone on the team as they develop at least three ideas to offer at the first problem-solving meeting.

The following case studies will show how the experts go about selecting interventions and accommodations that are tailor-made for each student referred.

Teacher Checklist for the Problem-Solving Process

- ❑ Make an appointment to see a coach

- ❑ Gather available data on the student
  - ❑ Work samples
  - ❑ Grades
  - ❑ Attendance
  - ❑ Cum file information
  - ❑ Other information as needed

During the referral conference:

Coach and teacher responsibilities

- ❑ Create "Strengths and Concerns" lists
- ❑ Conduct "Five Reasons Deep"
- ❑ Decide upon baseline information
- ❑ Set a DATA Goal and data collection strategy
- ❑ Select the team for the meeting
- ❑ Decide who will prepare the parent
- ❑ Decide who will make the follow-up call to the parent
- ❑ Decide who will prepare the student
- ❑ Set the proposed meeting time

- ❑ Prepare the student for the meeting
- ❑ Prepare the parent for the meeting

Expert team responsibilities

- ❑ Prepare and bring to the meeting, three low intensity interventions (one for home, one for school, and one for the student)
- ❑ Hold the meeting to create a plan
- ❑ Document responses and evaluate the effectiveness of the plan
  - ❑ Hold follow-up meetings to revise and refine the plan

Case Study–Elizabeth

Here is the information the referring teacher and Elizabeth's parents shared with the faculty "problem-solving experts" in order to help them design useful interventions for Elizabeth.

Elizabeth is a spirited first-grader who bubbles with energy but can lose herself in the moment, both verbally and physically. She has a tendency to attack classmates when she doesn't get her way. She has been known to shove people and call them "fancy" names. Sharing and taking turns are challenges for her. The students are beginning to band together and exclude her from playground games, lunch groups, and classroom teams unless an adult intervenes. Elizabeth has begun crying about coming to school, complaining of stomachaches, and tattling at least six or seven times a day.

Elizabeth is a high average achiever in all academic areas. She is creative and is not afraid to take initiative. When she wants something, she becomes a "girl on a mission" and is hard to derail. These leadership skills will serve her well if we can balance them with the social skills to make people want to follow her. Elizabeth loves her teacher and wants to please. She enjoys being a teacher helper. These traits will undoubtedly come in handy as ways to win her cooperation as we work on developing better social skills.

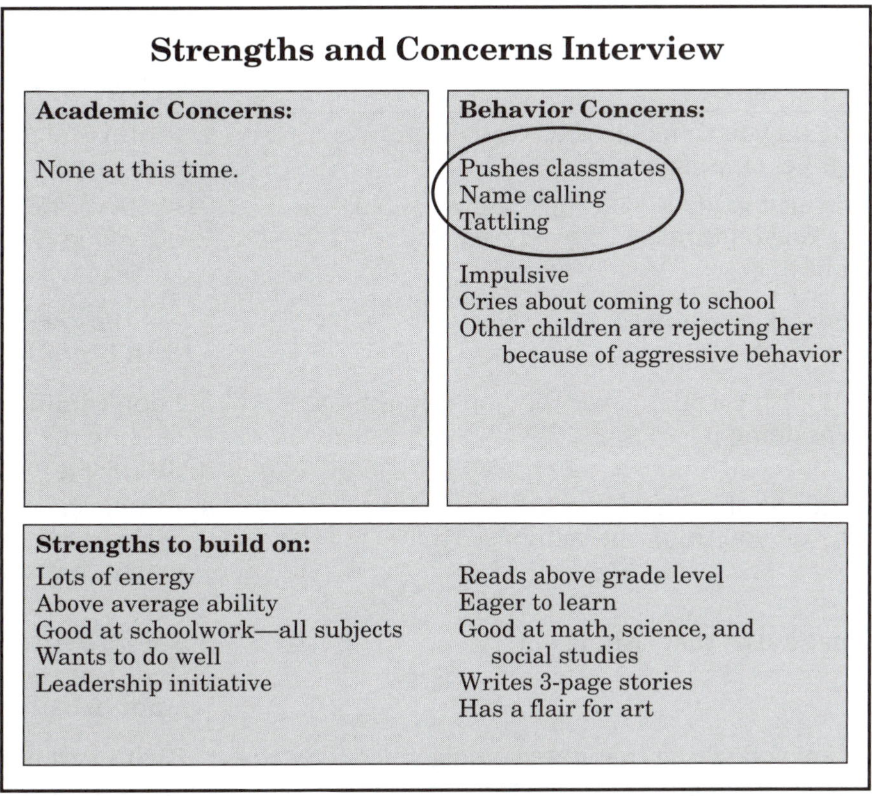

Strengths and Concerns Interview

Academic Concerns:

None at this time.

Behavior Concerns:

Pushes classmates
Name calling
Tattling

Impulsive
Cries about coming to school
Other children are rejecting her because of aggressive behavior

Strengths to build on:

Lots of energy
Above average ability
Good at schoolwork—all subjects
Wants to do well
Leadership initiative
Reads above grade level
Eager to learn
Good at math, science, and social studies
Writes 3-page stories
Has a flair for art

Potential "root cause" list developed by Mrs. Love (the art teacher and coach) and Mrs. Mikki (the counselor and problem-solving expert for students with poor social skills.)

Bored–Needs challenge, excitement and high drama fun.

Frustration–Over-challenged and stressed.

Focusing problems–She may not be paying attention to people's reactions, or perhaps she doesn't interpret people's intentions correctly.

Impulsivity–Does the first thing that comes to her mind without considering consequences. Not using reflective skills.

Inability to link with prior knowledge–Doesn't see a pattern of cause/effect and doesn't link her aggressiveness to how she feels when she is the victim.

Misplaced Anxiety–Anxiety about other problems or anger about things that are worrying her.

Retaliation for perceived injustices done to her.

Attention getting–Basic relationship needs not being met. Feels left out and uses inappropriate ways to connect with people.

Power seeking–Wants control over her world and takes it any way she can.

Coach says:	Teacher replies:
1. Why do you think Elizabeth is so aggressive with her classmates?	1. I think she is spoiled and just wants her own way.
2. Most first graders want their own way, but why do you think she's overly aggressive about it?	2. I believe she thinks the other kids will back off and give in to her.
* Is it working for her?	* No, the kids dislike her and don't want to play with her or have her in the group at all.
3. So if it isn't working, why do you think she keeps doing it?	3. I don't think she sees that she is the one causing the rejection. She thinks the kids are just being mean to her.
4. You think she doesn't see the cause/effect. Why do you think she cannot see that?	4. I think she only sees things from her side of the story. That's typical of her age to some extent, but she is extreme. She also just lashes out before she thinks.
5. What causes that lashing out?	5. She's a very impulsive child, and she just reacts and then cannot figure out why kids don't want her around.
* SO are you saying that if we could get her to slow down and get her to think before she reacts, she would make better choices?	* That's part of it, but I'm not sure she knows what those better choices are. Let's add that piece to the DATA goal.

DATA goal:

D—If we teach Elizabeth to stop and think before acting, and teach her how to make better social choices,
A—she will be able to participate in group activities with minimum conflict
T—within five weeks.
A—Growth will be measured by increased use of good social choices (see counselor's list), reduction of tattling to less than four times a day and reduction in name calling from an average of four times a day to no more than twice a day. Physical aggression will go to zero.

Baseline Data and Planning Form

Student Name *Elizabeth Yeats* Date referred *11/9* Referring person(s) *Mrs. Swartz*

Steps 1 & 2 - Key issues to be addressed*: *Tattling and aggressiveness with schoolmates*

Step 3 - Baseline data:**

Frequency: *Tattles 6–7 times a day. Physical or verbal conflict with peers - 4 times a day average*

Severity: *Kids totally exclude her from their groups*

Places problem is observed: *Unstructured places but sometimes group work in class*

Times when problem is observed: *Lunch, recess, phys. ed., mostly; sometimes in small group classroom work*

Things that trigger the problem: *When she doesn't get her way, feels threatened or left out. More apparent around Joe, Sharon, Tonisha, Eddie, Stephanie and Grace.*

Strategies that result in positive response: *"Cool-down corner," conference with parents, talking about good choices, ignoring tattles, pulling her behavior cards without scolding, clear classroom rules, and modeling.*

Strategies found to be ineffective: *Time-out as punishment, scolding, or shaming makes her angry and she fights back and escalates problem*

Reinforcements found to be effective: *Praise, fun time with peers, be the leader, teacher helper*

Reinforcements not recommended: *None*

Step 4 - DATA Goal: *** *If we teach Elizabeth to stop and think before acting, and teach her how to make better social choices, within five weeks she will be able to participate in group activities with minimum conflict. Growth in group situations will be measured by increase in good social choices, reduction of tattling to less than 4 times a day and reduction in name calling from an average of 4 times a day to no more than twice a day. Physical aggression will go to 0.*

Step 5 - Team members: *Counselor, first grade teacher, parents, Elizabeth, administrator*

Step 6 - Who will contact parents? *Mrs. Swartz*

Step 7 - Who will make the follow-up call? *Counselor, Mrs. Mikki*

Step 8 - Who will prepare the student? *Mrs. Swartz*

Referral taken by *Mrs. Love*

*Attach Strengths and Concerns form ** Attach work samples and observation data *** see "Five Reasons" document

Recording the summary and decisions on the Baseline Data and Planning Form helps the problem-solving experts focus on one aspect of a student's referral and prevents "Oops, I thought you were going to do that" communication problems.

Now it's time for each expert to select at least three ideas that will help Elizabeth "stop and think" as well as "make wise choices" (DATA goal).

What is typical for this age child?

One of the expert's duties is to know what is normal behavior for children of various ages. This puts the severity of the problem into perspective and helps the team make better decisions.

Complaining, tattling and bossing are common to most five and six-year olds.

Complaining, tattling, and bossing are common to most children in Elizabeth's age group, but Elizabeth's behavior is too extreme to be tolerated or just ignored. Six-year-olds typically are beginning to understand cause/effect to some extent. Most sixes are just starting to develop the ability to see things from another person's point of view. The expert uses this developmental information to guide the intervention selections.

Starting the process of developing interventions:

The first thing many experts do is ask themselves, "What do kids who do NOT have this problem think of that this child does not?" They are not looking for a list of what adults want the child to DO, but a list of ways other children THINK and solve problems differently. Another way to think of it is "what *mental models* do other kids have that Elizabeth does not?"

Mrs. Mikki, one of Elizabeth's problem-solving experts, considered what research taught her about impulsive children.

Impulsive children do not stop to consider, or even see, options other than the first one that pops into their heads.

Aggressive children often interpret neutral behaviors on the part of others as acts of aggression.

1. Kids who are not giving in to quick aggressive impulses generally have a better sense of "stop and think before you hit."
2. Impulsive children do not stop to consider, or even see, options other than their first thoughts when confronted by a challenging situation.
3. Other kids have learned things about taking turns and compromising that Elizabeth does not consider an option.
4. Some research says that children who cannot find words to express their anger have more of a tendency to strike out to show their feelings. This may be contributing to Elizabeth's problem.
5. Aggressive children often interpret neutral behaviors as aggressive. For instance, if I bump into your chair you can choose to believe I did it on purpose, even if I did not. Aggressive chil-

dren tend to jump to that conclusion more frequently than non-aggressive children.

6. Elizabeth may not be seeing the link between the pattern of how she treats people and how they respond to her later (cause/effect).

To help herself figure out which interventions would be helpful, Mrs. Mikki listed specific new "abilities Elizabeth needs" on a think sheet (see below). She used this list and her research database of ideas as the guide for selecting interventions and accommodations that match these needs. Since Mrs. Swartz had already carefully documented Elizabeth's responses to many basic interventions, Mrs. Mikki will be prepared to suggest more universal interventions but also some targeted interventions to extend Mrs. Swartz's effective practices. After looking at her database of ideas, Mrs. Mikki chooses several ideas to be done at home, at school, and for Elizabeth to do herself.

Recommendations for the first meeting

Root cause: Impulsive Behavior

Elizabeth needs to develop the ability to . . .	**Accommodations:**	**Interventions:**
1. Stop & think before acting. 2. Identify choices she could make. 3. Learn to do self-talk when angry. 4. Recognize when she is getting angry and do something to calm herself. 5. Figure out why the kids respond the way they do to her. 6. Learn when to share and compromise. 7. Use appropriate words to express her feelings. 8. Recognize if others have neutral intentions or bad intentions. 9. Learn to use words and actions that make people want to be around her.	1. Elizabeth will join a group working on social skills. 2. Use signal system to remind her to use the new skills. 3. Start a token system where Elizabeth has to give up tokens when she forgets to use her good skills. (1–3 Can be suggested for both home and school)	1. Elizabeth will track and analyze her own progress. 2. Elizabeth will help parents and teacher develop signals.

Research that guided Mrs. Mikki's recommendations:

One type of intervention based upon **social skill development studies** is the use of social stories (McGinnis & Goldstein, 1997; Kelly, 1997).

1. The teacher reads or makes up stories about good and bad behaviors based upon what the specific children in the group need to work on.
2. The teacher does think-alouds (verbalizing the thoughts) to model what she and other people in the story are feeling and considering as options.
3. Children identify appropriate and inappropriate behaviors and feelings.
4. The children practice in pairs and discuss how to treat others. This verbalization helps students internalize what they have learned.

To implement this social skills intervention, Mrs. Swartz will report Elizabeth's appropriate and inappropriate choices to Mrs. Mikki, the counselor. Mrs. Mikki will work with a small group of classmates to replay and revise what actually happens on the playground and classroom. This will allow Elizabeth and several other children who are having varying degrees of social problems to learn from their real experiences and discuss how they might make better choices in the future.

Teaching new skills is not enough. **Interventions are generally more effective when the child is taught to transfer the skills to a variety of situations.** (Rutherford & Nelson, 1988)

1. The new skill should be modeled by the adults.
2. Practice is scheduled with an adult who gives clear, timely and specific feedback.
3. Practice is scheduled with other students and analyzed for effectiveness.
4. New behaviors are observed as the student transfers the small group learning to the real situations. These observations are followed by specific feedback on strengths and suggested tips for improvement.

In Elizabeth's case, when the classroom and playground environments start showing progress, the team will slowly add the cafeteria, physical education class, and bus environments for transfer and practice of new social and behavioral skills. Skills are much easier to learn than they are to transfer, especially if there is a lack of ongoing support from teachers and parents.

Skills are much easier to learn than they are to transfer, especially if there is a lack of ongoing support from teachers and parents.

After practicing social skills in the group counseling session, the team knew application in a real situation would need close adult support and cueing. To accomplish this Mrs. Swartz and Elizabeth are to develop a set of signals to cue Elizabeth when she needs to calm down and rethink what she just did or was about to do. For example, the teacher would tap lightly on Elizabeth's desk as a signal that the pencil she just grabbed from Bobby was a violation of the "way we treat people" guidelines. If Elizabeth then remembered her new skill and went back and asked Bobby if it was OK to use his pencil, she could earn a green reward chip from the teacher.

Research shows that **corrective feedback has a powerful effect** on student achievement (Hattie, 1992). Elizabeth's feedback system was designed as follows:

The team decided to have Elizabeth track her own progress by giving her two sets of chips: four blue tattling chips, and one red chip for physical aggression. If Elizabeth wanted to tattle on a classmate, she would have to surrender a blue chip. If the teacher deemed the information important and not really a tattle, Elizabeth would get her chip back.

If Elizabeth could go through a day without losing any chips, the teacher sent home a Blue Ribbon Certificate letting her parents know that she had used her good friend skills. Ending the day with any blue chips at all allowed Elizabeth to choose from a menu of things she liked to do for the teacher (i.e., being a line leader for the highest number of chips and being the paper straightener for the least). Losing the red chip automatically made her ineligible for helping the teacher at all that day.

Two white chips were added after the second *successful* week to extinguish the name calling behavior. White chips could be earned for paying genuine compliments and using polite, friendly talk that made people feel friendly toward her.

The counselor had the "white chip" program going on with all the children in Elizabeth's social skills group. If Mrs. Swartz or a playground supervisor saw or heard Elizabeth or anyone in her group using "good friend skills," they would give the child a white chip (or mark the white chip symbol on the report paper). Children could also give each other white chips. The children would show these chips to Mrs. Mikki the next day and tell their success stories to the group. This was a friendship game with no tangible rewards attached to these chips.

Recess supervisors were in on the "chip" plan. Rather than carry the chips around, Elizabeth had a card with pictures of the chips that she gave to the supervising person. If she had to give up a chip on the playground, the adult would have Elizabeth explain why she had to cross out the appropriate chip on the card and then surrender that chip when she got back to her classroom. It is essential that all adults follow the plan exactly as specified, so as not to confuse Elizabeth. Inconsistency is worse than no plan at all!

This token system supported with short adult interactions acted as a quick, specific feedback intervention for Elizabeth. She charted her results each day to track her own progress. This chart would then be presented at the follow-up meeting to help everyone see how close Elizabeth came to meeting her six-week DATA goal.

Tokens Remaining	**Mon.**	**Tues.**	**Wed.**	**Thurs.**	**Fri.**
Blue—4					
Red—1					
White—2					
Rewards Earned					

During the course of the year Elizabeth showed great improvement in social skills. Mrs. Swartz was able to slowly fade the use of the chips by telling Elizabeth that she could now earn privileges without chips since she was showing respect for her friends and making good choices. Elizabeth's DATA goals were adjusted to include different issues and environments as she gained expertise in the initial skills. She did not require testing or an IEP because the assistance she received from the counselor's training (targeted intervention), the classroom teacher's ability to help her transfer the skills (universal interventions), and the support and practice her parents supplied at home did the trick. There was nothing easy about this effort, but many other children in the class ended up benefiting from the "good friend" practices, meetings, and discussions, even though they were originally designed to help Elizabeth and her group.

Mrs. Mikki has a list of other interventions waiting in the wings just in case the initial plan does not meet Elizabeth's needs. At first Mrs. Mikki thought developing this research database was labor intensive, but over the years, her work has resulted in a resource that is quite sophisticated. Being able to cut and paste ideas saves her tons of time.

Think Sheet For Powerful Accommodations

Root cause: Impulsiveness

Elizabeth needs to develop the ability to . . .

1. Stop and think before acting.
2. Identify choices she could make.
3. Learn to do self-talk when angry.
4. Recognize when she is getting angry and do something to calm herself.
5. Figure out why the kids respond the way they do to her.
6. Learn when to share and compromise.
7. Use appropriate words to express her feelings.
8. Recognize if others have neutral intentions or bad intentions.
9. Learn to use words and actions that make people want to be around her.

Accommodations: (adults do the most work)

1. Give her signals to cue her when inappropriate actions are being performed and she needs to slow down and think: count to five, deep breathing, self-talk, fix problems . . .
2. Stop incidents and have her tell what she could have done differently to get a better reaction.
3. Model good and bad examples of reactions and have the group critique and suggest alternatives.
4. Give the child pictures of situations and have her label the feelings and make suggestions for handling them.
5. Have the counselor "replay" incidents that have happened so Elizabeth can adjust her responses and discuss why she needs to.
6. Arrange to have a "cool down" place where Elizabeth can go when she is upset (time-out).
7. Have parents practice scenarios at home that she learned in school.
8. Spell things out for Elizabeth about appropriate and inappropriate actions and the consequences of each.
9. Play a game of "what would you do if . . ." to see who can make a choice that ends up making everyone happy.
10. Practice words and actions that help make friends. Keep track of how many times these ideas are used.
11. Play, "What do you think she was thinking" to identify possible motives.

Interventions: (student does the most work)

1. Have Elizabeth and peers analyze good and poor social skills and develop examples of good responses (use videos, role play, "what would you do if . . .").
2. Have her keep a picture journal of two good and two bad responses and how many times she uses each.
3. Have her develop stories where she and peers describe compromises they can make and how other people are likely to react.
4. Help Elizabeth ask for feedback from a trusted classmate on how she is doing on making people feel happy around her.
5. Have Elizabeth chart her behavior (tattling, name calling, and pushing) and have her analyze how she is doing and what plans she has for continuing improvement.
6. Have Elizabeth learn "self-talk" and new vocabulary to express herself and solve problems (i.e., How do you let people know you want to play?)
7. Have her write or draw the things she wants to tattle about and put them in a "worry jar" on the teacher's desk or tell her tattle to the teddy bear.

Case Study–David

Here is the information the referring teacher and David's foster parents shared with the faculty "problem-solving experts" in order to help them design useful interventions for David.

David is a sixteen-year-old ninth-grader who refuses to work. David has been in six different schools (including detention centers) and is currently living with his fifth foster family. His mother is deceased and his father is serving a life sentence for having killed her.

David is usually not a behavior problem unless he is publicly pushed to perform; then things can escalate quickly. Usually he starts out by responding to prods to work by saying, "Whatever." He then puts his head down on the desk and stays there. The most recent incident that earned a trip to the office was calling the teacher a bitch when she continued to push him to do his work.

David has only been in the school for four weeks and is already failing because he has done very little work: no homework and no written class work. Mrs. West is the only teacher who has seen a glimmer of hope in science class. After sitting in the back of the room refusing to do anything for two weeks, he unexpectedly joined a table of five classmates listening to a lecture on tape. David attempted to fill in the blanks on the study guide for the tape but then suddenly crumpled the paper and threw it away. Mrs. West was taken aback by the totally unreadable responses on the paper she retrieved from the wastebasket. David didn't appear to have even basic reading and writing skills. It was hard to tell where to start with him since no records were available from any former school, and David avoids showing teachers what he does and does not know.

His group of friends is a "Goth" group, and David assumes the leadership role in it. Other students distance themselves from David because of his threatening demeanor.

Strengths and Concerns Interview

Academic Concerns:

Unclear but likely to be early primary level for all reading, writing, and math skill

Can't see patterns

Doesn't link to prior knowledge

Lack of class participation

Behavior Concerns:

Refuses to work

Oppositional

Disrespectful

Volatile if confronted

Threatening to others

Doesn't believe in himself

Afraid to try

Strengths to build on:

Typical fluency in conversation

Enjoys music

Leadership potential

Takes initiative

Stands up for himself

High interest in motorbikes and cars

Able to speak in complete sentences

Oral grammar typical of his age

Root cause list developed by Mrs. Stevens (the administrator and coach) and by Mr. Knight (the counselor and problem-solving expert working with students who appear to be disrespectful and unmotivated).

1. Does the student need to gain power over his world in any way he can?
2. Is he seeking ways to establish his social place and forge relationships by appearing to be tough?
3. Is this about anger or revenge for being rejected by so many people?
4. Is he trying to avoid appearing to be a failure?
5. Does he want adult or peer attention (or both)?
6. Is he just taking the typical adolescent need to distance himself from adult authority too far?
7. Is he looking for ways to entertain himself through the thrill of pushing the limits?
8. Is he searching for ways to exercise his freedom to choose (typical of his age group)?
9. Does he refuse to try because he does not believe there is any chance of being successful with schoolwork?

David's behaviors are obviously attempts to fulfill his basic needs. Our job is to figure out which needs these current behaviors satisfy and replace his ineffective choices with new ones. Trying only to extinguish the negative behaviors could result in reduced motivation and uglier behaviors.

Coach says:	**Teacher says:**
1. Why do you think David refuses to work?	1. He seems to need to play tough guy and push people around.
* So you think refusing to work is his way of pushing teachers around?	* Yes.
2. Why do you think he does that?	2. Making yourself scary feels a whole lot better than showing your weakness and being ridiculed. Life has pushed him around. I think he is just plain angry at the world and scared of rejection.
3. We can't change what the world has done to him but we can make him feel safe and welcome. What do you think the academic issues are for non-participation?	3. Since he refuses to do much talking or working it is hard to say what his skill level is, but if what I saw two weeks ago is any indication, his skill level is on the primary level for reading and writing.
4. Why do you think his skills have remained so low?	4. There could be a long list of reasons. We don't have records to give us an I.Q. score and I'm not sure you could believe an I.Q. on a kid with so much emotional baggage anyway. He has been moved six times so who knows what kind of instruction he has had.
* So what assumption do you feel we can make with the information you do have on him?	* I can assume he doesn't have the skills to read on level and he may not be able to comprehend a lot of 9th grade content.
5. Why do you think he won't be able to learn the 9th grade content?	5. Because of a lack of vocabulary and background knowledge. That is most likely what is keeping him from trying.
* That sounds plausible. So you're saying making him feel safe and successful by providing the background knowledge and vocabulary will be our main focus?	* Yes, and helping him build success in his own eyes and in the eyes of his peers. It isn't cool to look like a loser.
* We will need to get him into an intensive reading/writing instructional program as soon as we can as well.	* I agree. It isn't going to take a ton of formal testing to see that this boy is on the critical list. Solid intensive instruction should be our first move, with all classroom teachers being on board to give him the chances he needs to build confidence in all classes.

D—If we teach David ways to successfully respond in class and build vocabulary and a solid knowledge base to hook new information to,
A—his motivation to participate in class will increase and he will attempt more work.
T—Within five weeks
A—he will attempt at least 60% of his written assignments as measured by a checklist kept by the teacher and David. David will participate 75% of the time (defined as: at least look at the teacher during instruction and respond when the teacher asks him questions privately).

An additional DATA goal in reading and writing is to be set as we are able to get baseline data on David's skill needs.

Baseline Data and Planning Form

Student Name *David Pathos* Date referred *9/14* Referring person(s) *Mrs. West*

Steps 1 & 2 - Key issues to be addressed*: *Lack of class participation and disrespectful attitude*

Step 3 - Baseline data:**

Frequency: *Daily refusals, disrespect when confronted, never agrees to actively participate in class*

Severity: *Does little written work, no public oral responses. Relates to no adults and a select few students. Reading and writing on a primary level.*

Places problem is observed: *All classes where grade level reading and writing is expected*

Times when problem is observed: *The attitude is pervasive but gets worse when he is pushed to do something that might show lack of skill.*

Things that trigger the problem: *Pushing him to perform in class, challenging his power to choose, kids who criticize or ridicule his action*

Strategies that resulted in positive response: *Letting him take his time, encouraging but not pushing*

Strategies found to be ineffective: *Confrontation, conferencing, contracts, calling foster parents*

Reinforcements found to be effective: *Choices of actions, easy oral tasks in small groups*

Reinforcements not recommended: *Grades, tokens, anything that makes him look different or exposes weakness in the eyes of peers*

Step 4 - DATA Goal***: *If we teach David ways to successfully respond in class, build vocabulary and a solid knowledge base to hook new information to, his motivation to participate in class will increase and he will attempt more work. Within five weeks he will attempt at least 60% of his written assignments as measured by a checklist kept by the teacher and David. David will participate 75% of the time (defined as: at least look at the teacher during instruction and respond when the teacher asks him questions privately.)*

Step 5 - Team members: *Mrs. West (Sc. Teacher), Mr. Knight (counselor), Mrs. Stevens (Adm.), David, foster parents, Mr. Roth (Soc Worker), Mrs. Wampler (Eng. teacher), Mrs Wood (Reading)*

Step 6 - Who will contact parents? *Mrs. West*

Step 7 - Who will make the follow-up call? *Mr. Roth*

Step 8 - Who will prepare the student? *Mr. Knight*

Referral taken by: *Mrs. Stevens*

*Attach Strengths and Concerns form ** Attach work samples and observation data *** see "Five Reasons" document

What's normal for adolescent behavior?

The need for power, relationships, and avoidance of looking like a failure are hallmarks of adolescent behavior. It is normal and healthy for David to protect his ego by refusing to look stupid in front of peers. David's present ways of satisfying these needs, however, are not healthy. Our job is to help him replace the choices he is presently making with choices that will reduce the bad side effects as he gains control of his world.

Revenge is an understandable reaction to all the blows life has dealt David, but this emotion will eat away at his potential. We need to help David learn coping skills as he continues to live a life none of us would wish for any child. David's behaviors will likely end up needing more intensive counseling interventions, but David's attitude toward counselors is less than positive at this point. It doesn't look like counseling sessions will be a productive choice for David until some groundwork is done to make him feel safe and welcome in the school.

Where should we start?

Mrs. Wampler is not only David's freshman English teacher, but also the problem-solving expert on **building motivation and helping kids feel safe in the classrooms.** The "Five Reasons Deep" interview helped her conclude that attention and entertainment were less important influences on David's choices than the first four root causes. Power, relationships, paybacks, and avoiding failure seemed to sum up David's underlying motivation.

Mrs. Wampler subscribes to the adage, "Believe you can or believe you can't; either way you are probably right." She knows that attitude tends to be a self-fulfilling prophesy. When tasks appear to be overwhelming, "I can't" is how the Davids of this world tend to think. Their internal talk goes something like this: "I can work really hard and get an 'F,' or I can put my head down, give the teacher the 'go away and leave me alone attitude' and get an 'F.' This is not a hard choice. If I don't have to stay in this room as a result of ticking the teacher off, that's a bonus. Decision made!"

Beginning with easier tasks that gradually get more difficult and complex results in less off-task behavior, unless the easy tasks result in boredom.

Intervention ideas for avoiding failure and increasing participation

Research: Beginning with easier tasks that gradually get more difficult and complex results in less off-task behavior, unless the easy tasks result in boredom (Flood and Wilder, 2002).

Mrs. Wampler needed to gather ideas that would make the work challenging, but not overwhelming for David. This will make it safer for him to participate. Here is the idea bank developed by Mrs. Wampler to help students gain confidence in academic classes.

Universal ideas for implementation in the general education setting:

1. Teach at least five key vocabulary words each week by using a variety of techniques (i.e., pictures, symbols, synonyms, paraphrased definitions, etc.)
2. Give the student a few "warm-up activities" that practice the skill of the day at a lower level at first and then move into more difficult versions.
3. Create worksheets that have the simpler questions or problems at the beginning and more complex things later. This taste of success encourages the student to continue working.
4. State questions in short simple sentences at first and let questions build in complexity as the student progresses.
5. It is important not to put too much print on a page for struggling readers.
6. Add visuals (graphs, pictures, diagrams, etc.) to coach the student through the initial problems, and fade the aids as skills increase.
7. Allow the student to work with a buddy for the first few problems or more through the more difficult parts of the assignment and then finish the rest of the paper on his own.
8. Supply the same information at an easier readability level or with a read-along tape.
9. Allow responses to be given orally, in person, or on tape, instead of just in written form, or allow students to orally redo the missed portions of written tasks.

Here are interventions that may require another adult's assistance (i.e., special ed, speech therapist, Title teacher, tutor, educational aide)

10. Give more support, such as modeling, tutoring, help to get started, feedback.
11. Front load or pre-teach the vocabulary and key concepts so when the student hears the full lesson in the general education room, he has prior knowledge and a study guide to make learning more effective.

Establish a prior knowledge base before the student is required to participate in a large group setting.

12. Go over advance organizers (notes, study guides, previews of material on video or audio tape) to establish a prior knowledge base before the student participates in a large group setting.

Mr. Knight is the guidance counselor and the expert on anger management and stress reduction. His job will be to add ideas that will help David gain a sense of power while minimizing the angry outbursts and disrespectful attitude.

Giving students choices within a structure helps them develop a sense of independence and responsibility.

Research: Teachers can do things that help students believe they can impact their world (Schunk & Zimmerman, 1997). For David, who has lived in a world that has been spinning out of control since he was small, gaining any kind of power is essential to his growth. Giving students choices within structure will help them develop a sense of independence and responsibility (Coopersmith, 1967).

Ideas for helping the student feel powerful through choices

Here are choices teachers can use in their general education rooms to encourage a discouraged and hostile learner:

1. Allow him to select a partner to work with if he wants to.
2. Give him choices as to the order in which he does assignments.
3. Select from a menu of topics to study within the scope of the curriculum.
4. Use some kind of signal so the teacher knows he does or does not want assistance. (green post-it on the desk, "I'm OK."–red post-it, "I'm stuck.")
5. Set his own gradually increasing goals for how much work will be accomplished in a given time period.
6. Allow him to hand in partially done assignments once in a while. None of us do our finest work every day. (Six good papers earn a "partial assignment" pass.)
7. Allow him to retake quizzes and tests when the grade is failing, to change a failing grade to at least C.

Ideas to curb anger

There is an old Native American adage: "Never try to catch a falling knife." This is a good thought to keep in mind when dealing with an emotionally-charged situation. Trying to confront a person in an emotional state is likely to result in an escalation of the situation. A pause in the action will probably be more productive.

1. Unless David is endangering himself or others, give him a moment to calm down before you have a conversation about what will happen next.
2. Say things like, "After class we can talk about how to solve this problem."
3. "Why don't you take a short time-out and write down or draw what you are upset about so we can talk when we have a moment."
4. Identify a calming down area where he can go and choose from several calming options (i.e., listen to music, use art materials, close his eyes and do deep breathing exercises, tear up newspaper, etc.)
5. Allow him to ask for a pass to go to the counselor's office for help.

Research: Self-monitoring, self-reinforcement and self-evaluation can enhance a student's ability to attend to task and eliminate behavioral problems (Zentall 1989; Digangi, Magg, & Rutherford, 1991). Helping David see the positive results of his effort by tracking his own successes in a visual way may help increase his motivation to keep trying even when things don't appear to be going well.

1. Set daily work goals and keep track of how many of them get done.
2. Score each of his assignments on a scale of 1–4. (1 = not attempted, 2 = attempted but incomplete, 3 = attempted and complete, 4 is complete and done well).
3. Teachers and David score assignments and then discuss how well their perceptions matched.
4. Teacher and David score and then both give one compliment for the work and one tip on how to make it better.
5. Chart progress on a graph (vocabulary words remembered, vocabulary words put into categories, number of math problems completed, points earned by accomplishing goals, etc.)

Tally every time you accomplish each task. Compare your chart to how your teacher tallied your work habits. Are you doing better than last week?					
David	**Mon**	**Tues**	**Wed**	**Thurs**	**Fri**
Starts work within 30 seconds					
Works for at least 4 min. at a time					
Completes assignment					
Looks at teacher during instruction					
Answers questions asked privately					

Ideas for improving Language Arts Skills

Feelings of hopelessness result in motivational paralysis.

Mrs. Wood, the reading specialist, is on David's team to help with the reading and writing issues. She knows that feelings of hopelessness result in motivational paralysis. People don't consider doing things they don't believe they can pull off. They often try to side-step embarrassment by avoiding the work. David's self-talk cannot be "this is too risky to try" if she expects him to participate and feel safe in the classroom environment.

Since he has minimal reading and writing skills, the intervention plan for science, math and social studies must focus on tasks that ease him into "safe" schoolwork. This probably means an emphasis on oral responses and adjusted reading assignments. Mrs. Wood will build in more complex tasks as David can handle it. At the same time, a parallel intervention plan will be used in the reading lab to work on teaching David to read and write for himself. He will be enrolled in a daily reading instruction program with Mrs. Wood that is designed to teach reading to adolescent learners with minimal skills.

If you are a teen, it is better to appear uncooperative and macho than stupid.

The scariest thing in the world for an adolescent is to be forced into a situation where his peers are likely to ridicule him. If accommodations are going to be made in the general education rooms, it is important not to make David look pathetic in the eyes of his peers by giving him watered-down work. His sense of self-respect will demand that he refuse the kind of help that makes him look inferior and different.

Ideas for overcoming reading and writing problems in content areas

Adding pictures and symbols to note taking makes the process more user-friendly.

1. Give the student recorded lectures to take to study hall or to take home for review or preview. This gives him a better chance of understanding things he might otherwise miss. (Tip: Only record mini-versions of lectures, five to seven minutes of highlights. Recording at home is far superior to trying to do this at school, because of the background noise.)
2. Teach the class to add pictures and symbols to their note taking. This is helpful for everyone and will allow poorer writers to employ a more user-friendly strategy.

   Pictures are remembered better than words alone.
3. Use partners or small groups to process information every five to ten minutes if possible. This keeps students involved and helps those who have fallen behind.
4. Roles in groups can be reader, recorder, illustrator or symbol maker, and checker. This gives poorer readers and writers opportunities to take part by assuming roles that are more compatible with their strengths.

Continuum of Intervention Levels to Support Academic Success

Along with an intensive reading program for adolescent non-readers,

David will start here ↓ | and work his way to these types of interventions as he transitions to general education classes ↓

	Concrete/simple: →			**Abstract/complex:**
Level of difficulty	Adult reads a simple version of the text and has David orally answer yes or no questions about the lesson. Give David notes before teaching the lesson and have him make symbols or pictures next to each key concept so he can retell the key lesson points using the notes. Pre-teach the vocabulary using pictures and context.	Adult reads and David answers multiple choice questions with two choices. He justifies his answer orally. Give David notes to follow as he listens to the lesson. Notes have the beginning letter in the blanks and a word bank. David fills in the notes and retells key lesson points. Match vocabulary to symbol cards.	Partner reads text and David creates symbol or key word on post-it notes to stick next to each paragraph. Worksheets have simplified text but all the key points. Visuals like graphs and pictures are added to assist with comprehension. He practices vocabulary before lectures or assignments with a partner as a warm-up.	Test starts with simple questions and gets more complex as it goes. David reads his own adjusted reading level material. Outline for lectures or reading has blanks for David to fill in with missing phrases. Studies his own vocabulary using a variety of strategies (matching, symbols, classifying, in context)
Level of support **(Can be a Person or Technology)**	**Teacher-led:** → Tutor front loads vocabulary and key concepts before David hears them in class. These vocabulary and key ideas can be practiced on computer to prepare for class.	David takes notes as he listens to a tape or a tutor. He adds symbols and pictures to these notes as he follows the lecture in general ed class.	David works with a buddy on the first few questions and finishes on his own, or starts by himself and finishes with a buddy. David verbalizes answers, buddy writes.	**Independent:** David takes his own notes and compares to a buddy or the teacher notes at the end of class. He could trade his notes for teacher notes if necessary at the end of class.
Size of task	**One-step:** → Teacher makes up a series of very short assignments rather than one long one. Length of assignment becomes longer and more complex as progress is seen.	David does some of the assignment in class and finishes with his tutor or at home. He can pre-do some of the assignment and finish in class.	Teacher breaks assignments into two or three parts and hands them out as previous work is completed.	**Multi-step:** David breaks his own assignments into smaller tasks and learns to take small breaks between tasks. He listens to taped lectures in small segments so he can take or review notes.
Type of feedback	**Extrinsic:** → David is given a free pass to skip an assignment or quiz if he completes a pre-agreed amount of work.	David may choose from a menu of rewards when he has two days of successful work completion.	David and a buddy can earn points for work completed and for work quality.	**Intrinsic:** David sets his own goals and tracks his own progress for both work completed and work quality.

The team knows that David will not be successful using only the ideas on the right side of the continuum chart, so they select things from the middle or left as their starting point. Their job is to move David as far to the right of the chart as they can each year.

The far left column is often delivered in a pull-out situation for a time with practice in the general education setting to allow for transfer of the new skills as soon as possible.

The second column tasks are often started in a pull-out situation but for less time and with more application in the general education setting right away. Special education teachers or reading specialists provide some accommodated materials to the general education teachers.

Moving to the right, the next column is generally implemented in the general education room and needs peer or direct teacher support, whereas the far right column involves less intensive intervention and is often used with a group of students in the general education room.

Because of the severity of David's reading problem, the team suggested going directly to intense reading interventions in Mrs. Wood's class, with general classroom accommodations giving him a second dose of language arts. Even though the interventions needed are intense, David will not need an IEP to get this instruction because the source of his reading problems appears to be lack of instruction, as opposed to a true learning disability.

Ideas offered at the first meeting

Root cause: fear of failure, need for power, inability to cope with anger

What new abilities does David need?

1. Tolerate and manage frustration.
2. Develop an "I can" attitude.
3. Find productive ways to gain freedom and power.
4. Develop ways to compensate for skill deficits while learning to read and write.
5. Learn to take notes so he can remember what he hears and reads.
6. Expand his speaking, listening, and reading vocabulary.

Accommodations: (Teachers and foster-parents do this:)

1. When David wants to argue, tell him when you can have this conversation, but don't have it right then. Teacher uses neutral face and voice to avoid escalating the problem and to send the message of being in control. After the incident, forgive and forget and start teaching good behaviors again.
2. Always correct David in a private location. Tell him the exact behavior you need to see.
3. Provide front loading of vocabulary and key concepts before the class lesson.
4. Provide remedial reading instruction using a computer assisted program.
5. Provide lectures on tape and templates for notes.
6. Assign reading or work partners.
7. Simplify worksheets.
8. Provide text material on David's level.
9. Give tests or parts of tests orally when needed.
10. Allow David to retake tests and quizzes he fails after being given an opportunity to study with a tutor.

Interventions: (David does these things:)

1. Learn to recognize anger before it erupts and choose a safe way to release it—counseling sessions first, then other venues.
2. List alternative actions you could have selected after making a poor choice.
3. Use a variety of note taking strategies to remember what is learned.
4. Re-tell key points of the lesson from notes.
5. Expand vocabulary using elaborative rehearsal techniques.
6. Track your own progress on setting goals and completing tasks.
7. Keep a checklist on how many times you participate in class and what type of participation it is.
8. Enroll in intensive reading program.

Case Study–Carmen

Carmen is a seven-year-old second grader with dark curls that bounce just like she does. Her big brown eyes let you know in a hurry whether she is happy or about to have a meltdown. Her intelligence is above normal, but her achievement is inconsistent from day to day.

Carmen's experience in pre-school was frustrating for both the teachers and for Carmen. She consistently had a difficult time following directions and complying with procedures and keeping her tantrums under control, which resulted in three changes in preschools.

As a kindergartner, the same pattern of poor achievement and conflict occurred and as school demands for attention to instruction increased, her lack of ability to keep herself focused and in control became more apparent. The teachers suspected an attention disability but Carmen's mother did not want her child labeled as special ed. The teacher made many accommodations to help with the attention problems (i.e., seating close to the teacher, frequent eye contact, quiet signals to keep her working, frequent feedback, and a token system that would earn special treats at home for good reports). All this resulted in very limited success.

In first grade, Carmen's doctor recommended medication to help her focus. The medication was adjusted several times throughout the year. As the medication level was being fine-tuned, Carmen's teacher continued using variations on the strategies from kindergarten and added a "time-out" space (not a cubicle) that served as a settle-down area. Carmen could choose to go to this area or her teacher could direct her to go. Carmen could choose to leave time-out as soon as she felt calmer. This system worked well on some days and had little effect on others. The teachers were compiling an increasingly clearer list of what worked and what did not work with Carmen.

The second grade teacher has come to the referral coach with the list of interventions tried and Carmen's response to each. Mrs. Harmon's strengths and concerns interview resulted in this list:

Strengths and Concerns Interview

Academic Concerns:	**Behavior Concerns:**
Language Arts:	Aggressive with others
75 sight words	Lack of attention to task
Little comprehension – main idea	Temper tantrums
Inference, drawing conclusions	Doesn't finish tasks
Math:	Gets out of seat and roams
Sequencing processes/starting	Does not make transitions well
No two-digit addition	
Trouble seeing patterns	

Strengths to build on:

Likes reading and math	Excellent computer skills
Wants to succeed	Strong visual memory
Likes teacher attention	Has an excellent vacabulary
Capable of second grade work	Is a dancer (ballet and tap)

Baseline Data and Planning Form

Student Name *Carmen Lopez* Date referred *11/24* Referring person(s) *Mrs. Harmon*

Steps 1 & 2 - Key issues to be addressed*: *Ability to begin and complete tasks, trouble with main ideas*

Step 3 - Baseline data:**

Frequency: *Carmen can't begin a new task 80% of the time without help. She stays on task for about 3 minutes. Her comprehension of main idea is on target less than 20% of the time.*

Severity: *Most children in class can begin within 20 sec. and stay on task for 8-11 minutes.*

Places problem is observed: *All academic classes, any transitions from task to task*

Times when problem is observed: *All day but much worse from right before lunch to dismissal*

Things that trigger the problem: *Changing activities or activities that take a long time or are difficult.*

Strategies that resulted in positive response: *Close to teacher, eye contact, frequent feedback, tokens, time-out when she chooses it as a cool-down place*

Strategies found to be ineffective : *Scolding, pairing with another student, time out as punishment*

Reinforcements found to be effective: *Art time, chances to move, get a drink, play a game, candy*

Reinforcements not recommended: *None*

Step 4 - DATA Goal***: *If we teach Carmen to begin her work promptly and lengthen her time on task, within three weeks she will be able to start work in a timely manner and concentrate longer. This will be measured by a chart showing an increase in work started within 20 seconds with minimal help and increase in time-on-task to 4 minutes. Her ability to identify the main idea of the lesson will increase to at least 50% of the time when asked orally as a result of being attentive.*

Step 5 - Team members: *Mrs. Harmon, Mr. Thornbury (spec ed.) , Mrs. Gribi (adm.), Mr. & Mrs. Lopez, Carmen*

Step 6 - Who will contact parents? *Mrs. Harmon*

Step 7 - Who will make the follow-up call? *Mrs. Gribi*

Step 8 - Who will prepare the student? *Mrs. Harmon*

Referral taken by: *Mrs. Siegel*

*Attach Strengths and Concerns form ** Attach work samples and observation data *** see "Five Reasons" document

Possible "root causes" developed by Mrs. Siegel (the psychologist and coach) and by Mr. Thornbury (the special education interventionist and problem-solving expert working with students who have attention problems):

Ability to focus and sustain attention on a given topic
Ability to control impulsive actions and reactions
Ability to comprehend and remember the sequence of information
Ability to recognize and generalize patterns
Ability to make smooth mental transitions
Ability to verbalize needs, wants, ideas and feelings
Ability to locate and use resources when needed
Ability to organize ideas and materials
Ability to visualize and verbalize steps in a task

Case: Carmen has problems getting work completed.

Coach says:	Teacher says:
1. Why do you think Carmen has difficulty completing her work?	1. I think it is a serious attention problem.
2. What causes Carmen's attention problems?	2. I'm not sure. She's on medication but she just can't get her work done.
3. Why can't she get it done?	3. About 80% of the time, she cannot seem to focus on where to start.
* If you get her started can she keep going?	* No, many times she just sits and stares at the paper or out the window. Other times she's up flitting around the room.
4. What do you think causes her to stare like that?	4. I am baffled by this. I have wondered if she is having mini-seizures.
5. We could ask the parents to check with the doctor. So you're saying that getting started is a problem. What keeps her from improving?	5. We've tried everything we can think of. She seems to need a jump start to get her going and the focus is gone after about three minutes. I don't think she knows how to focus herself.
6. So you want to teach her "getting started" strategies as well as how to focus herself?	6. Yes, but she is so severe, I think we need to start by having one-on-one modeling with someone. The documentation will certainly support that.
* I agree. Let's see if the team agrees to start at an intensive level.	

D—If we teach Carmen how to begin her work promptly and lengthen her time on task,
A—she will be able to start work in a timely manner and concentrate longer
T—within three weeks.
A—This will be measured by a chart showing an increase in work started within twenty seconds with minimal help and increase in time-on-task to four minutes. Her ability to identify the main idea of the lesson will increase to at least 50% of the time when asked orally.

Since pre-school, first and second grade teachers tried increasingly intense interventions with limited success; it is now time to go to a more structured model that gives Carmen even more support. The teachers will look at the options and try various interventions until they find one that works. Their goal will then be to bring Carmen down the intensity continuum as she shows improvement.

Mr. Thornbury's Continuum of Interventions and Accommodations:

Ideas from most intensive assistance to least intensive:

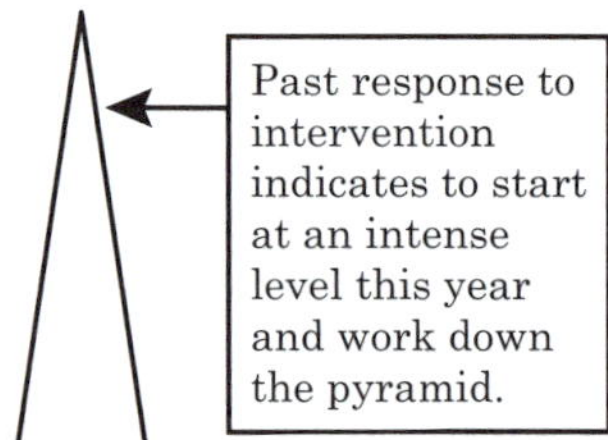

1. Have a special education teacher model the exact behaviors to be developed. Ask Carmen to describe the behaviors as the adult models them.
2. Ask Carmen to model while the specialist verbalizes a play-by-play of what she is seeing Carmen do. Adult gives corrective feedback if adjustments are to be made.
3. Carmen and a peer take turns, as one models and the other one describes the desired behaviors (adult observes and gives feedback).
4. Carmen models and describes or whispers the desired behaviors/steps aloud to herself. The adult gives feedback.
5. Carmen tries the same types of tasks in a general education room with adult support at first.

Breaking tasks down:

1. Carmen completes a small task paper to earn specific types of breaks (computer time, exercise break, art or listen to music break, etc.) with an adult right there to keep her going.

2. Carmen completes increasingly longer tasks to earn choice from the break list. Adult is cueing her to stay on task.
3. Carmen identifies how much of the work she can complete in a given amount of time on a longer paper. (Breaks it down herself into two parts.) The adult is close but not cueing her for on-task behavior unless absolutely necessary.
4. Given a list of tasks, Carmen schedules her own work and completes it with adult watching from a distance but not cueing her to stay on task.
5. When Carmen finishes tasks, she may go to the computer area on her own.
6. Carmen transfers this on-task behavior to a general education classroom—first with assistance and then without.

Ideas to help develop the ability to identify and access resources:

1. When Carmen gets stuck, the adult models how Carmen is to ask for help. Carmen then mimics the behavior.
2. When Carmen gets stuck the adult asks Carmen what she is supposed to do to get help.
3. The adult gives Carmen a silent cue that tells her to repeat the "what I should do when I need help" process.
4. Carmen can identify two things she could do to solve an "I am stuck" problem. One can be to ask a peer.
5. Practice this skill in a general education room with an adult to support but withdrawing that support and cueing as soon as possible.

Ideas for teaching transitions from task to task:

1. Adult models and verbalizes how to get ready to make a transition and how to get ready to start work once the transition is made.
2. Adult asks Carmen to describe the process, and then carry it out.
3. Have Carmen whisper the steps to herself as she performs them.
4. Adult asks Carmen to think through the steps and then show what to do.
5. On a cue, Carmen gets herself ready, transitions and starts to work. She and the adult verbally critique the process for quality. Carmen rewards herself for each step done correctly.

6. Practice transitions in a variety of settings (general ed., art, music, cafeteria, etc.) with an adult to support, but withdraw this support and cueing as soon as possible.
7. Give Carmen a "heads up" a minute or two before the transition is to be made so she has a moment to make a mental shift before she is required to move.

Ideas generated at the first meeting

Root cause: Inability to focus and make transitions

What new abilities does Carmen need?	**Accommodations:** (Adults provide crutches)	**Interventions:** (Carmen does most of the work and learning)
1. Start work in a timely manner without a prompt. 2. Work on a task for an extended time. 3. Stay in her seat until a task is completed. 4. Raise her hand to ask for help when she is stuck.	1. Carmen will have 30 min. practice sessions in the intervention resource room daily for two weeks. 2. A parent volunteer will be trained to help Carmen transfer these practiced skills to the general education room. 3. The teacher will design task papers that break down the second grade work into separate sheets that Carmen should be able to do in 4 min. or less. 4. The teacher/parent will model and describe the three behaviors to be worked on: getting started, staying on-task before taking a break (this is what it is and this is what it isn't), raising her hand to get assistance. 5. Token rewards will be given for following each step of the model. Her mother will reinforce with privileges if she gets at least 8 tokens. 6. Give Carmen a 'heads-up" 1 min. before time to make a transition so she can get ready. 7. Mother will model and practice these four things at home with fun activities—not on school work.	1. Carmen will help choose a strategy that will help her get herself started and stay on task. She will evaluate her performance at the end of the task and see if her teacher agrees with her assessment. 2. Carmen will tell the teacher how much work she can complete to earn special types of breaks (computer time, exercise break, art or listen to music break . . .) with adult right there to keep her going. 3. When Carmen gets stuck she will give herself a token if she remembers to ask for help, adult may cue her.

After two weeks of doing daily 30-minute practices in the special education room, there was some improvement for Carmen, but it was very limited. It was determined that Carmen needed more intense practice to get these behaviors in place well enough to transfer back to the general education setting. The plan was not changed but the intensity of the practice was. Carmen was to spend two hours in the resource room practicing her four behaviors while working on the same second grade work as her peers. She then practiced transferring those skills to the general ed. room for 30 minutes twice a day: during math in the A.M. and during science for 30 minutes in the P.M. Her art, music, PE, lunch and recess were still to be scheduled with her homeroom class.

After two more weeks the teachers were seeing real progress, but Carmen was having terrible problems in the fine arts areas, recess, and lunch. The plan changed to extending her time in the general ed. class to 45 minutes in the A.M and P.M but to have fine arts with a small group of children who also needed a tighter structure for these things. She also had lunch and recess with a group in a quieter more structured area. Social skills were to be introduced through games and fun activities in this setting. Carmen began to do much better.

The team decided that after monitoring Carmen's slow progress, even in this targeted and controlled environment, long-term intensive assistance would be recommended. The data collected from this carefully prescribed and documented intervention plan served as most of the multi-factored assessment and the eventual writing of the IEP. This RtI "response to intervention" data ended up getting the correct level of service for Carmen in a very timely fashion.

The team implemented the program that allowed incremental phase-in of Carmen operating with her peers in the general education rooms even though she continued to need support (skill transfer). Each new school year she seems to regress a little from where she ended the previous year. New kids, new schedules, and new teachers throw her world into a tizzy. Even vacation days can send her backward temporarily. Each time, the teachers up the IEP service intensity and then ease her back into more independent functioning with her peers. The team did not hesitate to adjust the IEP during the year to reflect Carmen's changing needs.

After the first month, the reading specialist was added to the team. Here is the list of accommodations and interventions she used to select the plan for improving Carmen's main idea and detail skills.

Ideas for teaching Main Idea and Detail reading skills

Level of difficulty	Concrete:	→	→	Abstract:
	Teacher demonstrates how to find the key idea in a single sentence or short paragraph. Student draws a symbol to represent the main idea. Teacher or student puts the word(s) next to the picture.	The student identifies the main idea and puts the key word or picture in the center of a web. He then chooses three important details from the selection and attaches these to the web's main idea.	Student uses post-it notes to identify the main idea of each paragraph in a short selection. He then uses the post-it note information to summarize the selection in his own words.	Student uses words or symbols to defend his steps and thoughts as he identifies main ideas and details and writes a summary of the passage.
Level of support	**Teacher-led:**	→	→	**Independent:**
	The teacher models how to select the main idea. The student then verbally describes how the teacher decided upon the main idea.	Student selects the main idea and defends his choice to the teacher. The teacher may have to use reflective questions to help the student get to this information.	Student chooses the main idea and defends his selection to a buddy. After hearing the buddy's idea and support for it, the student may change or stick to his original thinking.	Student works alone and is able to explain thinking processes with little or no prompting.
Size of task	**Simple one-step:**	→	→	**Multi-step:**
	Student identifies the main idea of a single sentence or picture.	Student identifies the main idea and three supporting details of a short selection or a picture. He then explains the basis for his selections.	Student identifies and supports his selection of the main ideas of several paragraphs and writes a short summary.	Student is able to identify and support his idea of the overall theme of a selection as well as several key ideas and their related details.
Type of feedback	**Extrinsic:**	→	→	**Intrinsic:**
	Teacher gives rewards or tokens that lead to rewards to student for viable responses to main idea practice.	Student self-evaluates his choices and teacher verifies and adds to the reflections. The teacher gives points and specific verbal recognition for work well done.	Student evaluates his work with a buddy's input and then gives himself a score. He gives himself extra points if his final evaluation matches the teacher's feedback. Teacher gives specific feedback to student.	Student self-assesses and defends his thinking about both strengths and weakness of his work. Teacher validates or adds insights. The student then sets his own goals for improvement. No direct teacher rewards needed in order to do quality work, although the teacher randomly may choose to do so.

Case Study–Courtney

Here is the information Courtney's parents, Miss Lockom (the librarian and coach), and Ms. Winston (the referring teacher) shared with Miss Histed (the faculty "problem-solving expert" for students with attention and memory problems).

Courtney is a bright, soft-spoken fourth-grader with a close circle of friends. She is consistently thoughtful and caring with her classmates, who presently seem quite concerned about the fact that she is so unhappy at school. For the last month she has been crying in class almost daily. Even though she reads fluently, she says she just doesn't understand most of the work and she hates school. Courtney's mother is getting the same story at home. Courtney has a stomachache every morning but seems fine after the bus is gone.

In class she is often inattentive, which explains much of her hit-and-miss knowledge. She daydreams and when called upon doesn't know what the question is. When she does answer, Courtney mumbles a few short vague sentences or sometimes goes entirely off the topic. When confused, she just copies what others are doing rather than ask for assistance. She seldom studies her notes, because they are sketchy and sparse. She works hard on papers, but something is just not clicking for her.

Strengths and Concerns Interview

Academic Concerns:	Behavior Concerns:
Language Arts:	Incomplete work
Poor writing and note taking skills	Highly distractable
Seldom answers in class	Lack of attention
Answers are brief and vague when given	Withdrawn/daydreams
Doesn't follow directions or even know what they are	Seldom asks questions
Math:	Doesn't like school
Doesn't follow procedures	Frustrated with school
Makes careless mistakes	Doesn't follow directions

Strengths to build on:	
Friendly and kind	Enjoys reading
Works well with others	Above average IQ
Memorizes well	Reading on grade level
Has close friends	Good reasoning ability
Gifted art student	Tries hard to do good work
Observant	Trains dogs as a hobby

Possible "root causes" developed by Miss Lockom (the librarian and coach) and by Miss Histed (the special education interventionist and "problem-solving expert" for students with attention and memory problems).

She doesn't have a clear idea of what is expected so she focuses on the wrong things.

1. She runs out of mental energy before the task is complete, and she doesn't know how to control the level of her attention.
2. The material is coming at too fast a pace or in big chunks that she is not ready to handle.
3. She doesn't believe she has a chance of being successful so she decides not to try.
4. She wants and needs attention and does not know a positive way to get it.
5. She wants power and sees this as a way to take it.
6. She has issues that are worrying her to a point of not being able to focus on anything else.

Courtney is crying in class

Coach says:	Teacher says:
1. Why do you think Courtney cries in class?	1. She isn't getting her work done.
2. Why isn't she getting her work done?	2. She's not retaining the information.
3. What do you think keeps Courtney from retaining the material?	3. She doesn't listen during class. She's OK with end of chapter questions, but everything else—she's in LaLa Land.
4. What's causing this daydreaming?	4. I don't know.
5. Let me give you some possibilities and see if anything rings true. Could she be distracted by something that is worrying her? Could she be sleep-deprived? Does she not know how to focus herself?	5. She's worried about not understanding her schoolwork but her mom doesn't think anything else is bothering her. We did talk about the sleep issue but her mom says, if anything, Courtney sleeps too much. I'm going with the focusing thing, but what can we do about that?
* Let's just write the DATA goal and see what the team comes up with. Do you think this will address both the academic and behavioral issues you selected?	* Yes, I think it is a possibility.

DATA goal:

D—If we teach Courtney to increase her ability to successfully focus her attention,

A—her ability to retain information will improve and her anxiety level will go down

T—within four weeks.

A—This will be measured by her ability to immediately restate what she just learned. Her anxiety improvement will be measured by weekly responses on an "anxiety rating scale" administered by her mother and her teachers. Ms. Winston, Miss Histed, and Courtney will design the scale together so we all know what we're looking for.

Baseline Data and Planning Form

Student Name: *Courtney Redding* Date referred *10/14* Referring person(s) *Ms. Winston*

Steps 1 & 2 - Key issues to be addressed*: *Ability to focus and cope with anxiety. Following directions on assignments.*

Step 3 - Baseline data:**

Frequency: *Daily crying and inability to pay attention (60% of the time)*

Severity: *She is getting D's in language arts, and social studies; F in math; C- in science*

Places problem is observed: *All classes but worse in LA, SS and math*

Times when problem is observed: *All day, even in cafeteria and playground she is withdrawn & sad*

Things that trigger the problem: *Any kind of verbal interaction—social or academic may trigger anxiety*

Strategies that resulted in positive response: *Having a buddy work with her*

Strategies found to be ineffective: *Reminding her to listen, calling on her when her hand is not up makes her freeze, giving her class notes to fill in*

Reinforcements found to be effective: *Nothing*

Reinforcements not recommended: *Using grades or points as incentives*

Step 4 - DATA Goal***: *If we teach Courtney to increase her ability to focus her attention, her ability to retain information will improve and her anxiety level will go down within four weeks. This will be measured by her ability to immediately restate what she just learned and again at the end of the class. Her anxiety improvement will be measured by weekly responses on an "anxiety rating scale" by her mother, her teachers, and Courtney. Ms. Winston, Courtney, and her mother will design the scale together so we all know what we're looking for.*

Step 5 - Team members: *Ms. Winston (teacher), Mr. Redding, Miss Histed (sp ed), Dr. Roberts (adm), Courtney, parents*

Step 6 - Who will contact parents? *Ms. Winston*

Step 7 - Who will make the follow-up call? *Dr. Roberts*

Step 8 - Who will prepare the student? *Ms. Winston*

Referral taken by: *Miss Lockom*

*Attach Strengths and Concerns form ** Attach work samples and observation data *** see "Five Reasons" document

Miss Histed's Think Sheet For Powerful Interventions and Accommodations

Root cause: Inability to attend or maintain focus

Skills needed to accomplish this goal:	**Accommodations:** (Adults provide crutches)	**Interventions:** (Courtney does most of the work and learning)
1. Ability to lengthen attention span. 2. Able to self-monitor for on-task. 3. Break large tasks into smaller ones. 4. Ask questions when lost or confused. 5. Learn when and how to take short mental breaks. 6. Link new idea to something meaningful. 7. Listen to and restate key points just learned.	1. Make a list of ways to take a mental break (draw a cartoon, close eyes and do relaxation exercise, walk to pencil sharpener, signal the teacher for a restroom break, practice deep breathing). Teacher practices with Courtney and they discuss the best times and places for taking these breaks. 2. Set a timer and a goal for work to be done. Play "beat the clock." Teacher checks for accuracy and work done. 3. Practice four strategies that sometimes help kids pay attention. Try each one for five or six days to see which works best. a. Beat the clock b. Cueing with a secret signal to get back to work. c. Teacher points to where she should focus on the page or puts a hand on her shoulder as a reminder to get back to work. d. Get a token for every four-minute period of good work and/or every task finished. 4. Daily practice of ways to ask for help when stuck. If she stops working, the teacher asks, "Are you stuck?" If yes, then ask "What will you do about that?" Have Courtney follow through on the plan to get help.	1. Teach Courtney to time her own on-task time and plot it on a graph. 2. Help Courtney design her own plan from a list of "things that help kids pay attention." 3. Ask Courtney to estimate how far she can work in a given amount of time and let her play beat the clock. 4. Have Courtney keep track of how many times she is confused and asks for help and how many times she does not. 5. Help Courtney make a list of "ways to take a short mental break." Have her check off which one she uses each time. Conference with her to see what she finds helpful. 6. Have Courtney take picture notes as she listens. Give her a column for symbols representing "How is this new idea like something you know?" 7. Ask Courtney to restate the most important part of the lesson she just listened to or the directions she just heard (to a teacher or peer).

After four weeks of trying several of these ideas, Ms. Winston became frustrated because there was absolutely no progress, even though Courtney did appear to be putting forth effort. During the next meeting Courtney's mother mentioned that Courtney's ear infections were flaring up again and that might have something to do with her ability to concentrate. The audiologist confirmed that Courtney's hearing was moderately impaired (at least for the moment), and she had had a great number of these episodes over the years. This called for a new plan. Lack of hearing doesn't get solved by motivating a student to try harder. At the second meeting, Miss Perez, the speech therapist was added to the team

The revised plan called for ways to help Courtney compensate for not always being able to hear the instructions or the lecture, especially in a large group setting. Miss Histed had read an article by Dr. David Sousa that explained the advantages of giving students time to reflect and process information about every five to ten minutes. This strategy would help all types of learners (universal intervention) and would be of special benefit to Courtney, as reflections and processing were done with a partner. Many of the things Courtney missed could be clarified without embarrassment as she held this summarizing talk with her partner.

Ms. Winston was advised by Miss Perez, the speech therapist, to move Courtney away from the noisy blower in the room. Courtney also agreed to use a personal FM system. This would allow her to hear what the teacher was saying even if the teacher's back were turned. Ms. Winston also made an effort to speak more distinctly and to look at Courtney as she gave directions. She tried to give instructions in brief segments with visuals to accompany her words whenever possible (gestures, overheads, models, chalkboard cues, illustrations, etc.). Giving Courtney written instructions as often as possible to avoid confusion was also suggested.

Another important point for the teachers to keep in mind is to avoid the temptation to give lengthy responses to a clarification question. Students with hearing losses do better with short sentences. Asking Courtney which parts she understood and then only re-explain the missed parts would make the process easier.

Courtney will keep track of her own progress. She will be able to restate what her assignments are and restate a key idea from the lesson to the teacher or a buddy.

Place a tally mark for each correct response to being asked to restate what she just learned or what the assignment is and a "?" for each time she is confused.					
	Mon	**Tues**	**Wed**	**Thurs**	**Fri**
Knows what the assignment is.	✔✔				
Knows at least one key idea from the class	✔??				

Jeremy is another student who was displaying similar symptoms to Courtney's. Miss Perez found that Jeremy's root cause was quite different than hers. While Courtney was having hearing difficulties, Jeremy's hearing was excellent but his ability to process what he was hearing was garbled.

Jeremy is a 13-year-old eighth grader with average intelligence. He is well-liked by peers and has a happy-go-lucky attitude about everything except school. He has a particularly difficult time with language arts and is presently getting an F in it. Jeremy learns better visually and has a talent for art but struggles in music class. When he has to listen, especially in large groups, Jeremy tends to get confused and lose focus. He is easily distracted by and sometimes upset by noisy environments.

What about Students with Auditory Processing Difficulties?

Some students who have auditory processing difficulties can repeat the words but still do not comprehend the meaning.

Unlike Courtney, students with an auditory processing problem generally have nothing wrong with their hearing, but their comprehension of what they hear is the issue. They generally have typical intelligence but have a developmental delay that causes distortion in the language part of their brain. This disability is one of the more difficult disabilities to identify because there are no reliable assessments at this time. The symptoms are similar to students with ADHD and Aspergers, but the types of problems it causes may not be consistent from day to day.

Courtney's team decided that having her paraphrase what she heard would be safer than just having her repeat the words she thought she heard. This would be even more important for Jeremy. Some students who have auditory processing difficulties can repeat the words but still do not comprehend the meaning.

It is important to teach students with hearing losses to take responsibility for their own communication needs as soon as possible. Courtney and Jeremy had to get used to not pretending that they heard what was said when they actually didn't. Feelings of negative self-esteem and anger are common for students with hearing losses and processing problems because the communication difficulties they experience make them feel like failures. These children often worry that others will become annoyed by being asked to repeat the conversation (Tye-Murray, 1998).

Students with auditory perception difficulties may have a hard time separating background noise from what needs to be heard (figure-ground).

Students with auditory perception difficulties may have a hard time separating background noise from what needs to be heard (figure-ground). Sometimes the problem is an inability to distinguish one sound from another. Difficulty remembering information received orally is another aspect of this problem. Sometimes the processing of words extends to written text as well as auditory information.

What teachers might report about students with auditory problems:

- Seems to have a hard time understanding words and meanings when being spoken to or when reading
- Speaks (or writes) in very short sentences or phrases
- Seems to have a hard time finding the words when speaking (and writing)
- Seems to ramble when speaking and is redundant
- Can only attend to spoken communication for a short period
- Distracted by background noise
- Cannot follow long conversations
- Hard time remembering things received orally
- Cannot distinguish some subtle sounds from others
- Needs more time to process oral information

Students with auditory problems often complain that:

1. Hearing is difficult when there is background noise. These background noises are also distracting.
2. Taking notes is troublesome because they miss many words when in a large and even in some small group situations.

3. Discriminating sounds of letters is difficult and can interfere with reading, vocabulary and spelling skills.
4. Paying attention to and remembering lectures, multi-step directions, lists and long conversations is exhausting and sometimes confusing.
5. Memory for auditory information may be weak.
6. Many also have organization difficulties.

The techniques that work well for Courtney often benefit a student like Jeremy, with auditory processing issues. Research is currently being done on such ideas as:

1. active listening strategies;
2. reduction in ambient noise;
3. reduction in complex verbal input (go slower, pause more, and increase volume slightly);
4. allowing more time for processing information received orally;
5. language-building exercises;
6. note-taking strategies that reduce information to the bare-bones version;
7. use of consistent routines and procedures;
8. teaching these students to take responsibility for solving some of their own problems: ask for help, avoid noisy areas for work, write things down that will be easily forgotten.

Here is Miss Perez's continuum of ideas for helping students with auditory learning problems:

Level of difficulty	**Concrete:** →			**Abstract:**
	Adult models good speaking and response patterns. Student mimics and paraphrases the process. Teach vocabulary that will lengthen responses. (Transition words; therefore, because, for example.) Teachers use "wait time" to give the student time to process information.	Adult models and the student describes what is being modeled . . . Student then repeats what is learned and verbalizes in his/her own words as the work is done. Ask mostly "Yes", "No" and multiple choice questions.	Student whispers the main ideas or steps as the task is performed. Student asks or signals when the teacher needs to slow down or repeat things. Ask questions that require short answer responses. Give directions in writing or picture form.	Student seats self where he/she can hear and see best. Student uses earplugs when needing to screen out distracting noise. Student may check with a friend to be certain he/she understands each step or main idea before beginning a task. Assign homework buddies so student can call to get clarification.
Level of support **Person or technology**	**Teacher-led:** →			**Independent:**
	Therapist works on extended verbal responses and helps with lip reading and sign language. Use speech technology to assist if needed.	May need a personal FM system in classes. Sp. Ed. teacher front loads the lesson for student. Student practices asking for help when confused.	Teacher tapes the lectures so student can review on his/her own and catch the things missed. Someone else takes notes so student can process; highlights notes afterward.	Uses advanced organizers and checks notes with a partner several times during class. Teacher gives entire class this opportunity.
Size of task	**One-step:** →			**Multi-step:**
	Verbal instruction and directions are kept very short and checks for comprehension are made after each segment of each lesson.	Verbal input is kept to a moderate length and checked for comprehension at the end of each segment.	Verbal input is given with accompanying visual cues when there are multiple steps or lengthy messages.	Student breaks down assignments or learning periods into manageable chunks and takes little mental breaks when needed.
Type of feedback	**Extrinsic:** →			**Intrinsic:**
	Student is given tokens for giving increasingly longer answers, and for asking for assistance when confused.	Student gives self tokens for increasingly better answers and self-directed behavior.	Student uses a checklist to monitor own improvement and compares self-assessment with the teacher's observations to validate.	Student self-assesses and develops own suggestions on how to improve or what new goals will be.

Case Study–Carl

Here is the information Carl's parents, Mr. Guy (the math teacher and coach), and Mr. Kaufman (the referring teacher) shared with Miss Leggett (the special education interventionist and "problem-solving expert" for students with organization problems).

Carl is a seventh grader in middle school. He is very well liked by his peers. In fact, because he is so insightful and knowledgeable, students seek him out as a partner, especially in science class. He has a good sense of humor and has excellent computer and music skills. He has 140 IQ so he is capable of completing seventh grade work but seldom finishes it. When he does finish, it often gets lost before it is handed in.

Carl typically walks into class without paper and pencil. His notebook looks like a trashcan with papers sticking out from all directions. Throwing anything out is something that seldom occurs to Carl. His last on-task audit revealed that he spends almost half of his time messing around. He has a hard time sitting still and his follow-through on directions is very poor. Carl can be argumentative with the teacher when asked to get back on task.

Carl goes from one extreme to another when it comes to attention. Most of the time he gets bored with the task and quits, but when he does get involved with something that catches his interest his teachers have a difficult time getting him to transition to the next activity.

When Carl completes his written work, the quality is generally poor. The only thing that saves his grades is consistently high scores on tests. The teachers' main concerns are: poor writing skills, incomplete work, and being argumentative. After the "five reasons deep" interview, Mr. Kaufman decides to focus on teaching attention to detail and organization skills as the root causes to focus on first.

Strengths and Concerns Interview

Academic Concerns:

Language Arts:

Poor writing skills

Lack of detail in assignments

Cannot stick to a topic

Math:

Doesn't show work

Doesn't do all steps

Behavior Concerns:

Off-task behavior

Very disorganized

Argumentative

Incomplete work

Poor quality of work

Doesn't connect cause and effect

Does minimum

Highly distractible

Doesn't have materials

Disruptive in class

Strengths to build on:

Very bright and articulate

Wants to do a good job

Good support at home

Loving family

Has music talent

Strong computer skills

Brilliant science student

Very well liked by peers

Very funny sense of humor

Possible "root causes" developed by Mr. Guy (the math teacher and coach) and Miss Leggett (the special education interventionist and "problem-solving expert" for students with organization issues).

Cannot get started and then maintain attention to tasks

Cannot filter out distractions

Poor sequential memory

Fine motor difficulties interfere with writing

Inability to pace activities

Cannot separate key ideas from details

Boredom

Cannot visualize patterns

Impulsive behaviors

Doesn't have a clear idea of what the end product should be before he starts

Inability to self-monitor

Does not see the relationship between his effort and what happens to his achievement

Difficulty classifying and categorizing information

Coach says:	Teacher replies:
1. What is keeping Carl from getting his work done?	1. He just doesn't try.
2. Why does he refuse to try?	2. He's not refusing to try, he's just careless with his work and materials.
3. What causes this careless attitude?	3. I wish I knew. Maybe he's just lazy.
4. Some kids who look lazy are really frustrated, so they give up. Others haven't learned to pace themselves so they run out of time.	4. Frustrated is not it. Carl has a very quick mind. Pacing is a problem, but I think it's deeper than poor planning. It's like no planning skills at all.
5. What is keeping him from planning?	5. What do you mean?
* Things like inability to sequence tasks, lack of attention to detail, inability to sort and categorize.	* Absolutely! Every one of those sound like Carl. In fact, lack of sequence and detail is exactly what is wrong with his writing and math. Lack of sorting is why he cannot find his assignments. That's perfect. Let's start with those organization skills.

DATA goal:

D—If we help Carl learn to organize his ideas and materials
A—he will be able to complete and hand in higher quality written work
T—within four weeks
A—as assessed by: having his materials organized at the beginning and end of each class as defined in the checklist at least 80% of the time. His work will be completed and turned in at least 70% of the time with a minimum grade of C.

Baseline Data and Planning Form

Student Name: *Carl Machino*   Date referred *10/22*   Referring person(s) *Mr. Kaufman*

Steps 1 & 2 - Key issue to be addressed: **Lack of focus and organization skills*

Step 3 - Baseline data:**

Frequency: *Turns in work 45% of the time. Average score on writing rubric is 1 out of a possible 4 points. Disruptions in class about 50% of the time, math grades average D-*

Severity: *D's all subjects except science. Class disruptions are joking and soft but consistent talking. Only stays on task for about six minutes. Loses his assignments about 30% of the time. Comes unprepared for class about 75% of the time*

Places: *All classes unless he is very interested (i.e. science..hands on . . .) better if task is verbal or done in a group*

Times when problem is observed: *Math class and any written assignment in all classes*

Things that trigger the problem: *"Boring" work, written work, rote work, math problems, writing spelling words, copying, extended responses*

Interventions that resulted in positive response: *Partner with a smart, attractive girl as a study buddy*

Interventions found to be ineffective: *Organizing materials for him, giving him a rubric for organization, giving him a timer to time himself*

Reinforcements found to be effective: *Earning time on the computer*

Reinforcements not recommended: *Grades, detention*

Step 4 - DATA Goal:*** *If we help Carl learn to organize his ideas and materials, he will be able to complete and hand in higher quality written work within four weeks as assessed by: having his materials organized at the beginning and end of each class as defined in the checklist at least 80% of the time. His work will be completed and turned in at least 70% of the time with a minimum grade of C.*

Step 5 - Team members: *Mr. Kaufman (teacher), Miss Leggett (spec ed), Mr. O'Brien (administrator), Carl, parents*

Step 6 - Who will contact parents? *Mr. Kaufman*

Step 7 - Who will make the follow-up call? *Mr. O'Brien*

Step 8 - Who will prepare the student? *Mr. Kaufman*

Referral taken by *Mr.Guy*

*Attach Strengths and Concerns form   ** Attach work samples and observation data   *** see "Five Reasons" document

Mr. Guy's bank of interventions and accommodations for learning to sequence things and ideas:

1. After reading a story, put the picture cards of the events in order and retell the story.
2. Copy and extend patterns with beads, geometric figures, motions, numbers (e.g., X, O, XX, O, XXX, O . . .)
3. Learn to play chess, checkers, or any game where figuring out the pattern determines success.
4. Sequence a "to do" list and put the amount of time you think it will take next to each item.
5. Verbalize the sequence of a science investigation and explain what effect changing the order might have on the outcome.
6. Mix up a set of directions for making something. Try doing the task with the mixed up directions first, and then re-order the directions in the proper sequence.
7. Have the student create "How-to cards" that enumerate each step of a process he finds difficult to remember, such as how to get ready to start class, how to file your papers at the end of class, and how to do each step of a math problem.

Ideas for organizing a work area and materials:

1. Be very clear about what "good" looks like and what will not be acceptable. Use pictures and words to describe the criteria.
2. Have a buddy help organize papers or materials. The buddy will model the thought process aloud and the student will repeat the step-by-step process as he follows through (Shevits, Weinfeld, Jewler & Barnes-Robinson, 2003).
3. Color code "to do cards," folders and papers to each subject so the student keeps things together that go together.
4. Carl will use pictures or a diagram of what an organized desk and folder look like. He will grade himself every day as to how his desk and folder looks at the beginning and end of class.
5. Carl will organize his homework file every day before leaving school and when he completes homework at night.
6. When Carl has mastered a given organization skill he may act as a tutor or mentor for a younger child who is having the same type of difficulty.
7. Quickly re-teach at least one organization skill at the beginning of every class ("Do you remember where your finished

papers go? Tell me." "What needs to be inside your math folder right now?")

8. Have the student use the checklist to critique someone else's work area or folders and give one compliment and one tip for improvement.

Ideas for managing time:

1. Give the student an agenda for the day so he can see where the lesson is going and how he needs to pace his work. Help him set up a daily schedule for accomplishing tasks.
2. Put the same number of rubber-band bracelets on the student's left wrist as he has tasks to do. Have him remove each rubber-band as each task is completed and handed in.
3. The student will break large tasks into smaller, less overwhelming segments, especially if they are long-term assignments.
4. Have the student tell the teacher when he feels he understands an assignment well enough to not have to complete rote assignments. If he can prove this by doing seven examples, he may skip the rest of the assignment.
5. Put a red X on the paper where the student may stop and take a short break. Start out with a short amount of work and lengthen the amount of work that must be completed as the student improves.
6. Have the student make his own estimate of how far he can be on a given assignment within a given amount of time. Have him track his progress as he is able to do more work in a shorter amount of time.

Task to help students organize ideas:

1. Provide the student with written organizers like webs or partial outlines prior to class so he can actively follow the lesson by filling in the organizer.
2. Teach the student to write down ideas in a variety of note-taking styles (including picture and symbol notes) so he learns to process and reflect as he listens.
3. The child can work with a student checker (someone he can ask to verify whether he has followed all the steps) before handing in work.
4. Have the student brainstorm ideas for something he plans to write and then eliminate extraneous information and add details to his outline before he writes.

5. Color code main ideas with a yellow highlighter and key details with a second color.
6. Classify vocabulary or key ideas, name each category, and defend your grouping pattern.
7. Use a variety of graphic organizers to visualize how information fits together.
8. Use rubrics and checklists to self-monitor.

Ideas to manage behavior in class:

1. Teachers will spell things out in terms of disruptions they cannot live with. Be specific about what it looks like and sounds like.
2. Build in legitimate times during class when the student is allowed to move around without causing a disruption.
3. Make certain the student is looking at you and listening before giving instructions. Walk close to him and put a hand on his desk, if necessary (Ford, Olmi, Edwards, & Tingstrom, 2001).
4. The student will develop a contract for improvement and keep data of his progress on a graph. He will revise his plan as determined by his success rate.

Mr. Guy's ideas to present at the first meeting

Root cause: Organization skills

(What new mental skills are needed?)	Accommodations: (Adults provide crutches)	Interventions: (Carl does most of the work and learning)
1. Ability to lengthen attention span 2. Ability to organize his thoughts before writing 3. Ability to sequence and organize work, time and materials 4. Increase ability to find work and turn it in on time 5. Ability to pace activities 6. Ability to sort and categorize information and materials 7. Ability to attend to and verbalize details	1. Teachers will model good organization and develop a diagram that will show Carl exactly what that looks like. At the beginning and end of each class the teachers will simply point to the picture of how his materials should look as a cue for him to get to that point quickly. 2. The teacher will take three pictures of materials ready for class: a perfect desk, a little less perfect, and a totally unacceptable desk. Carl and the teacher will use hand signals to decide if his desk is in 1, 2, or 3 condition. 3. Parents will give points for every night that all homework arrives home with the needed materials and points for having all completed papers in the homework file.	1. Carl will be able to get his materials ready for class and organize his materials and papers in time to leave class. 2. Carl will monitor his own progress for organization of materials at home and at school and compare his assessment to the adult assessment. 3. Carl will color code each subject's folder. 4. Give Carl the option of having a buddy check his organization before having the teacher look at it—as long as the buddy is one who is trained not to do the work for Carl.

As with any struggling student, the critical starting point for Carl was to make him believe that he could learn to be a better organized person. He needed to understand that people are not just born organized. Organization is a matter of learning a series of tricks and steps that work for a specific person in a specific situation. If he would be patient with himself and us, he could select the exact tricks that would work for him.

The team decided that Carl's initial instruction in organization would be with the general education and the special education teacher. Carl would be sent to the resource room for "organization and on-task lessons" for 30 minutes a day for two weeks where he would see models and have plenty of opportunities to practice the new skills. If successful, he would then go to the organization classes every other day and report on how his new skills were working in the general education room (Fatata-Hall, 1998).

At first Carl only monitored his ability to be ready to start and end the class. The teachers were very specific about what would constitute "ready to start class."

Rule 1. Be in your seat when the bell rings, quiet and with materials ready. (Carl was given an aerial-type drawing of where the pen, pencil and book should be on his desk).
Rule 2. Be ready to leave one minute before the bell rings (Work turned in, papers in correct folders).

"x" means no point for that time segment	**Monday**		**Tuesday**		**Wednesday**		**Thursday**		**Friday**	
	Begin	**End**	**Begin**	**End**	**Begin**	**End**	**Begin**	**End**	**Begin**	**End**
1st Period										
2nd Period										
3rd Period										
4th Period										
5th period										

After Carl began to show significant progress on the organization skills, the teachers added criteria for behavior. After the first few sentences of explanation, students tend to shut down, especially if the discussion begins to sound like a lecture, so the teachers explained in very concise and clear terms what would be expected and what would not be tolerated during class time in order to get points in each category. The need to be firm and consistent about following through is critical to the success of any point (token economy) program.

"x" means no point for that time segment	**Point for being ready to start class**	**Point for each 15 minute period with no talking at the wrong time**			**Point for each 15 minute period without joking at the wrong time**			**Avg. minutes on task per period**
1st Period								
2nd Period								
3rd Period								
4th Period								
5th period								

After making certain that Carl knew exactly what the expectations were, the teachers agreed on a hierarchy of consequences that would be dealt out if there were violations of these basic rules. Consequences were not presented as punishments but ways to get the student's attention. (The teacher should always use the gentlest way that works. No sense raising the roof when raising an eyebrow would do the job).

For example:

Rule 1. Be in your seat when the bell rings, quiet and with materials ready.
Rule 2. Raise your hand when you wish to speak.
Rule 3. Work until the task is finished or for seven minutes, whichever comes first. If you need to take a short break after seven minutes, do so quietly and then get back to the task until it is finished.

Consequences within a given period:

First violation gets a signal to get ready within the next five seconds.

Second violation gets an "x" on the tally sheet instead of a point.

Third violation is a change of desk closer to the teacher.

Fourth violation gets a desk by the teacher for a longer period of time.

Research has shown that self-regulation and monitoring strategies help students evaluate their own progress and on-task behavior. Systematic communication between the regular education and special education teacher also helps transfer the skill from the small practice session to the larger venue (Rooney, Hallahan, & Lloyd, 1984).

This self-monitoring is a strategy to use after the teachers have modeled exactly what is meant by on-task behavior and off-task. Once the student can consistently identify the behaviors to the teacher's satisfaction, the self-monitoring begins. On a cue (usually a beep on a tape recorder used with headphones) have the student ask himself a question like, "Was I paying attention?" or "Am I following my plan?" The student records his yes/no response on a tally sheet and immediately gets back to work. This tallying usually takes place every 20–30 seconds for 20 minutes.

The weaning process. After the habit of self-monitoring is in place, the student is instructed to continue keeping track of his on-task frequency on his chart but without using the tape. This happens for five or six days. The next step is to tally the on-task behavior mentally rather than on a tally chart (Hallahan et al., 1982).

What if the intervention doesn't work?

I am often asked, "Well, what if none of our interventions work?" If none of the interventions worked, it means the adult's work is nowhere close to being finished. The question, "What if nothing works?" operates the same way in medicine as in education.

If nothing works you have two choices: give up or keep trying.

The give up scenario has grim consequences. Most of us hope our own doctor doesn't take this attitude with our family members. We cannot afford to do that in education either. Instead, we need to consider where our original plans went wrong. Could it be that we need to bring in a new team of advisors? Did we carefully work our way up the levels of the continuum and try things that research says typically work but we have never considered before? Perhaps we had the wrong diagnosis and were working on the wrong DATA goal.

"It just didn't work," is not an acceptable stopping point. "It just didn't work," is where we kick in the afterburners and go at the problem in a new way. As stated in the film *Apollo 13,* "Failure is not an option." It's not that we won't fail at times, but failure should not be a stopping point. It should be considered a sign that we have not gone far enough. "Stinkin' Thinkin", as Dr. William Perkey has been heard to refer to it, sets us up for failure. We may have little or no success in meeting our goals at times, but it shouldn't be because we didn't pool all our forces and talents in order to give it our best efforts.

> Men who try something and fail are infinitely better than those who try nothing and succeed.
>
> Lloyd Jones

Intervention Continuum Chart

Level of Difficulty	**Concrete:** → Teacher demonstrates using concrete materials or examples as the student mimics the process observed.	Student uses concrete materials or examples and describes each step to the teacher.	Student uses pictures and/or symbols as he explains the process to the teacher orally.	**Abstract:** Student uses words or symbols to defend his steps and thoughts as he solves problems using the skills taught.
Level of Support	**Teacher-led:** → Teacher models and student verbally describes the modelling observed.	Student does the work and responds to teacher's prompts, cues or reflection questions.	Student works with buddy and explains the step-by-step thinking process.	**Independent:** Student works alone and is able to explain thinking processes with little or no prompting.
Size of Task	**Simple one-step:** → Task requires one step thinking or use of a single skill to solve a problem.	Task requires two steps or two skills used together to solve a problem.	Task requires three steps or three skills used together to solve a problem.	**Multi-step:** Task requires 4 or more steps to complete or transfers the use of skills to an unfamiliar situation.
Type of Feedback	**Extrinsic:** → Teacher does out-loud feedback as student works each step or Teacher provides reinforcement or rewards for good student work.	Student reflects upon work as teacher guides and adds comments. Teacher and student agree upon goals required to qualify reinforcements. Teacher gives rewards.	Student reflects upon work with a buddy. Student gives himself a reward if he can justify that he met requirements.	**Intrinsic:** Student self-assesses and defends thinking about both strengths and weakness and sets his own goals for improvement. Doesn't need teacher rewards to keep working.

Glossary

Accommodations Aids and supportive crutches that help minimize the damage of a problem situation or disability.

Baseline data Information collected at the beginning of the referral process that paints a clear picture of the starting point for a student. This data is then compared to the same data collected every six weeks (or more frequently) to see if the intervention is working or if it needs to be modified.

Circle of Influence Keeping the discussion focused on things over which you have control.

Chunking Clustering information into logical and learner-friendly size bits in order to help students make connections, see patterns and not become overwhelmed with information.

Continuum of Interventions A series of strategies designed from least intrusive to most intensive to address a specific student's need. The team incrementally moves up the continuum if less intensive strategies fail to meet the student's needs. Once a level of strategies is found that works, the team moves the student down the continuum as he gains skill.

DATA goals Targets written to guide the intervention plan that clearly spell out the following things:

1. What the adults will do **D**ifferently
2. What new **A**chievement this will enable the student to perform
3. The **T**ime in which this intervention should show this achievement
4. How everyone will be able to measure and **A**ssess the degree of success of the intervention plan.

Elaborative Rehearsal Practice that takes advantage of the brain's ability to store information in multiple places, thus enhancing its ability to retrieve information later. Studying is done using multiple sensory modes (verbal, visualization, kinesthetic, music) to process information more deeply than using just one style.

Expert Pool Faculty members who have devoted their professional development time to becoming an expert on a specific type of learning or behavior problem.

Five Reasons Deep Analysis The discussion between the coach and the referring person that looks beyond symptoms to see what makes this student's way of learning different. Digging out the root cause of the problem.

Front loading The process of pre-teaching the vocabulary and key concepts before hearing this information in a general education room. This gives students a fair playing field and helps prevent parts of their brain from shutting down because of elevated stress levels.

IDEIA Individuals with Disabilities Education Improvement Act, 2004.

Interventions The treatments that result in putting new skills in place that help the student become more self-sufficient. Interventions help students cope with or do things on their own even if a support person is not available.

Pyramid of Interventions The federal guide that shows how a student population should be served in order to overcome barriers to learning. 80–90% of the students could be served successfully if quality Universal Interventions were used in every classroom. 5–10% of the students will still need additional support beyond what a master teacher can supply in a general education classroom. 1–5% of the students will need intensive interventions with ongoing support in the general education classroom to enable these students to transfer their new skills to other environments.

Referral coach Persons on the faculty who have been trained in active listening and diagnostic questioning. The coach guides the analysis discussion to identify the root causes and then assists in designing a DATA goal (a specific, short-term, measurable target for change).

Response-cost program A strategy where points are lost for breaking previously established rules. Points remaining may be turned in for privileges or rewards. These procedures should only be used for the most disruptive behaviors and only when the adults managing the strategy have been carefully trained. Consistency is essential for success.

RtI Response to Intervention The aspect of RtI used in this book is the multi-tier or pyramid system of options (Tier I, II and III). The level of interventions tried starts at low intensity and based upon data collected carefully moves up until the intervention selected is the lowest intensity that works for this individual.

Root Cause Looking beyond symptoms to find the barrier at the heart of the problem. This is the issue that keeps a child from learning and performing to his maximum capability.

Self-monitoring The ability to track and assess your own progress and determine goals based upon this data.

Strengths and Concerns Interview The beginning conversation with the coach in which the referring person identifies the key symptoms that worry the adults as well as strengths this student already has in place.

Time-out Removing students from the positive reinforcement of classroom activity to a neutral environment for a short pre-set amount of time. This is only effective when the classroom activity is desirable to the child; it is not effective if the child wants to avoid work. At the end of the time-out, the teacher and student discuss ways to prevent this problem in the future.

Token Economy A strategy where students earn tokens or points for improving academic or social positive behaviors. These points may be exchanged at the end of a day for rewards or privileges.

Transitions The ability to move seamlessly from one task to another.

Universal Interventions Powerful strategies that, if implemented well, would prevent most students from experiencing frustration in a general education classroom.

Bibliography

Adelman, H.S., & Taylor, L. (1998). Reframing mental health in schools and expanding school reform. *Educational Psychologist, 33*(4), 135–152.

Caine, R.N., & Caine, G. (1991). *Teaching and the brain.* Association for Supervision and Curriculum Development.

Darch, C., & Carnine, D. (1986). Teaching content area material to learning disabled students. *Exceptional Children, 53,* 240–246.

Druckman, D. & Sweets, J.A. (1988). Enhancing human performance: Issues, theories, and techniques. Washington, D.C.: National Academy Press. In E. Jensen. *Teaching with the brain in mind.* Association for Supervision and Curriculum Development.

Fatata-Hall, K. (1998). Acquisition and application of study skills and test taking strategies with eighth grade learning disabled failing social studies. From ERIC Document Reproduction Service No. S0029064

Flood, W.A., & Wilder, D.A. (2002). Antecedent assessment and assessment-based treatment of off-task behavior in a child diagnosed with attention deficit-hyperactivity disorder. (ADHD). *Education and Treatment of Children, 25,* 331–338.

Hallan, D.P., Tarver, S.G., Kauffman, J.M., & Graybeal, N.L. (1978). A comparison of the effects of reinforcement and response cost on the selective attention of learning disabled children. *Journal of Learning Disabilities, 11,* 430–438.

Hattie, J., Biggs, J., & Purdie, N. (1996). Effects of learning skills interventions on student learning: A meta-analysis. *Review of Educational Research, 66*(2), 99–136.

Healy, J.M. (1990). *Endangered minds: Why our children don't think.* New York: Simon & Schuster.

Jensen, E. (1998). *Teaching with the brain in mind.* Association for Supervision and Curriculum Development.

Kelly, C.R. (1997). *Improving student discipline at the primary level.* Master's Action Research Project, Saint Xavier University, and IRI Skylight Field-Based Master's Program. (ERIC Document Reproduction Service No ED412007)

LaBerge, D. (1995). *Attentional processing.* Cambridge, MA.: Harvard University Press.

McGinnis, E., & Goldstein, A.P. (1997). *Skillstreaming the elementary school child.* Champaign, IL: Research Press.

McTighe, J., & Wiggins, G. (1999). *Understanding by design.* Association for Supervision and Curriculum Development.

Nuthall, G. (1999). The way students learn. Acquiring knowledge from an integrated science and social studies unit. *Elementary School Journal, 99*(4), 303–341.

Pascual-Leone, J. (1970). A maturational model for the transition rule in Piaget's developmental stages. *Acta Psychologica, 32,* 301–345.

Pressley, M., Symons, S., McDaniel, M., Snyder, B.L., & Turnuer, J.E. (1988). Elaborative interrogation facilitates acquisition of confusing facts. *Journal of Educational Psychology, 80,* 268–278. In R. Marzano, D. Pickering, & J. Pollack (2001), *Classroom instruction that works.* Association for Supervision and Curriculum Development.

Rooney, K.J., Hallahan, D.P., & Lloyd, J.W. (1984). Self-recording of attention by learning disabled students in the regular education classroom. *Journal of Learning Disabilities, 17,* 360–364.

Rutherford, R.B., & Nelson, C.M. (1988). Generalization and maintenance of treatment effects. In J.C. Witt, S.N. Elliot, & F.M. Gresham (Eds.) *Handbook of behavior therapy in education* (pp. 277–324). New York: Plenum Press.

Silven, M. & Vauras, M. (1992). "Improving Reading Through Thinking Aloud" *Learning and Instruction. 2*(2), 69–88.

Shevits, B., Weinfeld, R., Jewler, S., & Barnes-Robinson, L. (2003). Mentoring empowers gifted/learning disabled students to soar! *Roeper Review, 26*(1), 37–40.

Smith, Rick. (2004). *Conscious classroom management: Unlocking the secrets of great teaching.* Conscious Teaching Publications.

Squire, L. R., & Kandel, E. R. (2000). *Memory from mind to molecules.* New York: Scientific American Library.

Sugai, G. Horner, R.H., & Gresham, F. (2002). Behaviorally effective school environments. In M.R. Shinn, H.M. Walker, & G. Stoner (Eds.), *Interventions for academic behavior problems II: Prevention and remedial approaches.* Bethesda, MD: National Association of School Psychologists.

Tye-Murray, N. (1998). *Foundations of aural rehabilitation: Children, adults, and their family members.* San Diego, CA: Singular.

Vargas, A.U., Zentall, S.S., & Wilbur, J.D. (2002). Responses to art attention-training by English and bilingual Spanish-speaking students with and without ADHD. *Studies in Art Education, 43,* 158–174.

Walberg, H.J. (1999). Productive teaching. In H.C. Waxman & H.J. Walberg (Eds.) *New directions for teaching practice and research* (pp. 75–104). Berkley, CA: McCutchen Publishing Corporation.

Wolfe, P. (2001). *Brain matters.* Association for Supervision and Curriculum Development.

Zenall, S.S. (1986). Self-control training with hyperactive and impulsive children. In J.N. Hughes & R.J. Hall (Eds.) *Handbook of cognitive behavioral approaches in educational settings* (pp. 305–346). New York: Guilford Press.

Zentall, S.S., & Kruczek, T. (1988). *The attraction of color for active attention problem children. Exceptional Children, 54,* 357–362.

Index

About the Authors

Margaret A. Searle

Margaret A. Searle is a nationally known education consultant in the area of collaboration, problem-solving, and innovative teaching techniques. She is the author of Ohio's state training manuals on standards-based instruction and collaborative problem-solving, and has spent many years as the lead trainer for statewide seminars on "Leadership for Results."

Her professional experience includes ten years of teaching in all grades K–8, three years as a middle school principal, seventeen years as an elementary principal, and three years as a K–12 supervisor. She is past President of the Ohio Association of Elementary School Administrators (OAESA), and has served as an education advisor to President George H. W. Bush. Margaret is the author of the Ohio Department of Education's Treasure Chest book on standards-based instruction and co-author of the National Early Childhood Education Standards.

Currently, Margaret is President of a consulting firm based in Perrysburg, Ohio. She is a national consultant in the areas of curriculum/assessment mapping, standards-based instruction for at-risk learners, team problem-solving, and differentiated instruction.

Dr. Karen Ackerman-Spain

Dr. Karen Ackerman-Spain is a Licensed Psychologist working with children in a clinical setting for approximately twenty years. She is also a Licensed Clinical Counselor, certified to teach elementary education and special education. Karen is also an Assistant Professor at The University of Findlay in the College of Education. She has presented at both national and international conferences regarding intervention strategies for students diagnosed with mental health issues in the general education classroom.